T0311668

A Short History of Disruptive Journalism Technologies

A Short History of Disruptive Journalism Technologies provides a swift analysis of the computerization of the newsroom, from the mid-1960s through to the early 1990s. It focuses on how word processing and a number of related affordances, including mobile-reporting tools, impacted the daily work routines of American news workers.

The narrative opens with the development of mainframes and their attendant use as databases in large, daily newspapers. It moves on to the "minicomputer" era and explores initial news-worker experiences with computers for editing and publication. Following this, the book examines the microprocessor era, and the rise of "smart" terminals, "microcomputers," and off-the-shelf hardware/software, along with the increasing use of computers in smaller news organizations. Mari then turns to the use of pre-internet networks, wire services and bulletin boards deployed for user interaction. He looks at the integration of decentralized computer networks in newsrooms, with a mix of content-management systems and PCs, and the increasing use of pagers and cellphones for news-gathering, including the shift from "portable" to mobile conceptualizations for these technologies.

A Short History of Disruptive Journalism Technologies is an illuminating survey for students and instructors of journalism studies. It represents an important acknowledgment of the impact of *pre-internet* technological disruptions that led to the even more disruptive internet- and related computing technologies in the latter 1990s and through the present.

Will Mari is Assistant Professor in the Department of Communication, Northwest University, USA. He is a media historian and interested in how technology impacted the lives of news workers, especially marginalized groups such as women and minorities, in newsrooms during the twentieth century. He received his Ph.D. from the University of Washington, USA, and his MPhil from Wolfson College, Cambridge, UK.

Disruptions: Studies in Digital Journalism
Series editor: Bob Franklin

Disruptions refers to the radical changes provoked by the affordances of digital technologies that occur at a pace and on a scale that disrupts settled understandings and traditional ways of creating value, interacting and communicating both socially and professionally. The consequences for digital journalism involve far reaching changes to business models, professional practices, roles, ethics, products and even challenges to the accepted definitions and understandings of journalism. For Digital Journalism Studies, the field of academic inquiry which explores and examines digital journalism, disruption results in paradigmatic and tectonic shifts in scholarly concerns. It prompts reconsideration of research methods, theoretical analyses and responses (oppositional and consensual) to such changes, which have been described as being akin to 'a moment of mind blowing uncertainty'.

Routledge's new book series, *Disruptions: Studies in Digital Journalism*, seeks to capture, examine and analyse these moments of exciting and explosive professional and scholarly innovation which characterize developments in the day-to-day practice of journalism in an age of digital media, and which are articulated in the newly emerging academic discipline of Digital Journalism Studies.

www.routledge.com/Disruptions/book-series/DISRUPTDIGJOUR

A Short History of Disruptive Journalism Technologies

1960–1990

Will Mari

Routledge
Taylor & Francis Group

LONDON AND NEW YORK

First published 2019 by Routledge

2 Park Square, Milton Park, Abingdon, Oxon OX14 4RN
605 Third Avenue, New York, NY 10017

Routledge is an imprint of the Taylor & Francis Group, an informa business

First issued in paperback 2022

British Library Cataloguing-in-Publication Data
A catalogue record for this book is available from the British
Library

Library of Congress Cataloging-in-Publication Data
A catalog record has been requested for this book

ISBN: 978-0-815-36791-8 (hbk)
ISBN: 978-1-03-233859-0 (pbk)
DOI: 10.4324/9781351256247

Typeset in Times New Roman
by Apex CoVantage, LLC

Contents

Figures

Acknowledgments

I should first thank Matthew Kirschenbaum for his encouragement, both from his example and via his friendly tweets, for some of the ideas that follow. Specifically, for the need to write about how rank-and-file journalists encountered word processing, I am indebted. Also Brian Creech, Juliette De Maeyer, Susan Keith and Noah Arceneaux, both in correspondence and in person at conferences such as ICA and AEJMC, provided helpful suggestions and feedback, and inspired me with their smart and perceptive research. Creech and De Maeyer, with their use of materiality in journalism studies, aided my thinking about how news workers conceived of, and used, technology, including how they spoke about such tools in their workplaces (newsrooms) and how they worked together to resist and/or adopt the technologies in question. Keith and Arceneaux, with their examination of newsroom-production tools and cellphones, respectively, inspired me to look at discrete technologies and their contexts – devices arose from specific needs in specific times and places.

I would be remiss if I did not thank the friendly archivists and librarians at the Living Computer Museum in Seattle, including the brilliant Marie Williams Chant and Dorian Bowen, for their help and access to emulator software, working machines and their increasingly relevant and vital archive of software documentation and manuals from the 1970s and 1980s. They helped me think through how institutions such as news organizations would have acquired software during the Cold War, trained their staff on them, and then also incorporated different proprietary programs and hardware into work routines. The librarians at my university's library, including Adam Epp and his staff, were also instrumental in helping me acquire secondary texts (and in some cases even buying them!). My other colleagues at Northwest University, including Clint Bryan, Chrystal Helmcke and Renee Bourdeaux, were also kind enough to lend me their suggestions and encouragement during the long and sometimes hectic research and writing process. My graduate-school companions and now fellow communication studies scholar-colleagues, including Courtney Johnson, Matt Bellinger and Miles Coleman, spent some of their valuable time reading and commenting on elements of my project while they were still very rough indeed. Thank you, friends. Christopher Lim and Corey Kahler, truly faithful friends and both programmers, also helped me think through the details of software and hardware. Our student worker in the Department of Communication Studies at Northwest University, Tiani Grosso, helped to transcribe a number of articles in the latter stages of research, and another student worker, Marissa Johnston, assisted with locating relevant technology ads in the early stages of research.

My former dissertation advisor, Richard Kielbowicz, remains an encouraging sounding board. It was he who originally suggested that early word processing programs and dedicated video-display terminals would be worthy of study as a sequel project to my book on the history of American newsroom culture. He very generously lent me thousands of copies of trade publications from the 1950s through the 1990s, especially *Editor & Publisher*, *Columbia Journalism Review*, and *Quill*, but also miscellaneous (and hard to acquire in bound, physical form) copies of ANPA *Research Bulletin*, *Newspaper Research Journal*, and clippings, reports and various other material that he has collected over the years.

Bob Franklin, the insightful and innovative Disruptions series editor, who first approached me about contributing, was incredibly kind and encouraging throughout the process. It was he who, while editing *Journalism Studies*, first thought my article in that publication deserved a longer and more detailed successor, and advocated for its inclusion in book form in this series. I should also thank Kitty Imbert and the staff at Routledge for their valuable assistance with preparing the manuscript for digital publication.

Finally, my wife, Dr. Ruth Moon Mari, in the midst of finishing her own dissertation, helped me from the beginning with practical suggestions and constructive critiques. Her love and brains got me through another book project, and it is to her that this monograph is dedicated. Thank you, Ruth!

Abbreviations

AFL-CIO	American Federation of Labor and Congress of Industrial Organizations
AFP	Agence France-Presse
ANG	American Newspaper Guild
ANPA	American Newspaper Publishers Association
ANPA RI	American Newspaper Publishers Association Research Institute
ANPAT	American Newspaper Publishers Abstracting Technique
AP	Associated Press
ASNE	American Society of News Editors
ATF	Bureau of Alcohol, Tobacco, and Firearms
CLASS	Classified Ad Storage and Sorting Program
CPI	Consumer Price Index
CRT	cathode-ray tube
DEC	Digital Equipment Corporation
IBM	International Business Machines Corporation
INTREX	Information Transfer Experiments
IRE	Investigative Reporters & Editors
ITU	International Typographical Union
MS-DOS	Microsoft Disk Operating System
NIOSH	National Institute for Occupational Safety and Health
OCR	optical character recognition
PC	personal computer
PDP	Programmable Data Processor
RI	Research Institute
SDC	Sigma Delta Chi
SPJ	Society of Professional Journalists
TTS	Teletypesetter
UPI	United Press International
VDT	video-display terminal

1 Introduction

Toward a history of disruptive journalism technologies

Before the internet and the computer, newsrooms and news workers[1] were wired and mobile.

But when I began research for this monograph, my initial conceptualization of newsroom computerization,[2] including the use of pre-internet networks and mobile-tech adoption by news workers and in newsrooms,[3] was to think of separate, if parallel, technology tools, that is, the car, telephone, fax machine, telegraph, scanner, and so forth. These, though, I naively realized later, operated alongside one another and then came together in the period from the 1950s through the 1990s when the advent of the civilian internet early in the latter decade meant, in time, nothing less than the transformation of journalism.[4]

Now, having read through much more of the journalism trade literature of the latter Cold War, I have come to the humbling conclusion that a more holistic, earlier-than-expected computer-centric approach would be more appropriate. The use of the computer by newsrooms was disruptive, but not in the ways I had thought. Newspapers, large and small, adopted computers as part of centralized minicomputer/video-display terminal (VDT) systems, used fax machines to send optical-scan-readable news copy as part of wire-service networks and dispatched reporters to political conventions and sporting events to send back their stories via modems and acoustic couplers in sophisticated and pioneering ways. Computers were expensive, bulky and often available initially to only the largest news organizations, but present, and in use, throughout the 1960s, 1970s and 1980s.

One of this project's chief contributions, then, will be to show the uneven, but early, computerization of the newsroom across a range of news-gathering and news-curation and news-producing activities from the mid-1960s through the early 1990s. News workers used pre-internet databases and networks and at first proprietary, then more off-the-shelf (i.e., ersatz), software and hardware systems, with operating systems and network software (i.e., MS-DOS and UNIX) that both previewed use by the wider public but also paralleled developments in the software industry. As information workers, journalists used computers to report the news, store it and share it with others. They did not exist, of course, in a vacuum of singular circumstances, but were themselves a force and a factor in the history of hardware and software in American businesses.

Their role, then, as early adopters of computers for their occupation is worthy of study, but also interesting in and of itself as part of the larger story of journalism and technology.

Sources/inspirations

This study borrows from the literature of science and technology studies, journalism studies, the sociology of work, and other related social-science fields. While other scholars, notably Matthew Kirschenbaum, have explored the use of the word processor and computer in contemporary literature, few others have touched explicitly on the use of computers in journalism during the latter Cold War.[5] A major focus of this study will be on how word processing impacted the daily work routines of American news workers, but even this fundamental technology will be examined alongside a number of related affordances, including mobile-reporting tools.

This study also responds to calls for a "materiality"-infused approached to media-history research, in which things and tangible technologies form a major part of the story(ies) of adoption, resistance and change.[6] While devices such as cameras, cars, telephones and typewriters are examples of material objects and tools influencing and even radically alternating news work, I will argue that the hardware and software associated with newsroom computerization was at least as impactful on news work as the aforementioned machines combined.

Looking, then, at the use of such tools in the pre-internet era is helpful in understanding the present and even the future (cautiously), as it shows the long tail of development and context for present-day technologies. Mobile reporting, for example, did not emerge in the 2000s, but had been present since at least the mid-century, if not before.[7]

I should mention at the outset what this project is *not*, in addition to what it *aspires* to be. It is not an exhaustive history of the computer in the newsroom, though it is among the first to examine the computerization of the newsroom, during any era. It is not a history of word processing or any other explicit genre of software, though, following Kirschenbaum's example, specifics will be included wherever possible. I am not a historian of computing, nor a computer scientist, and my training and theoretical orientation draws from my identity as a media historian and journalism-studies scholar, but I am agnostic and open to approaches from sister fields. Furthermore, this is not a history of software alone (though software that edited text and executed basic layout functions will be mentioned fairly extensively). I will not cover extensively the growth of various Videotex and Teletext services that arose and then faded in the 1980s. These ancillary technologies are important precursors to the internet, but did not directly concern most news workers. This is, finally, not a study of newspaper production technologies per se. These are defined as the printing, distribution and other "making" processes of the newspaper plant. For that I defer to my colleagues Susan Keith and Juliette de Maeyer (among others).

Instead, I am chiefly focused on news-gathering, initial editing and curation technologies associated with and powered by the computer, such as those encountered and used by the typical news worker in North America (and to a lesser extent, the United Kingdom and Canada) in the latter Cold War. This is a survey of those analog and early digital antecedent tools used by news workers and the news industry, and that led up to the even more disruptive internet- and related computing technologies in the latter 1990s and through the present. It covers Cold War-era computing and related tech tools that came before but influenced those that came after.

So why stop at *c.* 1990?[8] And why start with the 1950s and 1960s? By covering the immediate period that led up to the internet, I cover *pre-internet* technological disruptions of and within journalism, of which there are enough and which have enough impact on the field of journalism to deserve their own separate, sustained attention – not least of which is an examination, which I attempt briefly, of the computerization of the newsroom.

To the best of my knowledge, there is no such study available in English at this point, though I hope more will follow. Following in the path of such cultural historians as Robert Darnton and, within the realm of media history and sociology, Michael Schudson, I have attempted a "thick" description of events whenever possible and also tried, if haltingly, to write an initial and broad narrative of how computers came to the newsroom. By looking at those devices, along with early networks, I hope to provide critical context on the further disruptions brought by the internet.

Context on Cold War computing and the newsroom

A number of scholars have examined the recent history of the impact of technology(ies) on global newsroom cultures, including the disruption and evolution of work routines, journalistic authority, role changes, and engagement with audiences, among many other subjects. The general trend has been to complicate, rather than to simplify, "the role of technology in how journalism works," as Matt Carlson has framed it succinctly.[9] Indeed, "past generations of news workers confronted the implementation of new newsroom technologies with an array of contradictory reactions, from the assuredness of continuity to fear of disruption to the hopefulness of reinvention, before they became an unnoticed part of how news was created."[10] Henrik Örnebring has explored the up-skilling, de-skilling and reskilling of reporters in Scandinavia and in Europe with the arrival of the internet, as has Nikki Usher and Mark Deuze, in newsroom culture in the United States.[11] Kevin Barnhurst and John Nerone have similarly examined how technologies (plural!) have impacted how news is gathered and produced.[12] But going back to the seminal studies of Gaye Tuchman, Herbert Gans, Mark Fishman, but also Leo Rosten and Warren Breed, other scholars were intrigued by what technology, and specifically the computer, were doing to journalism and its practices.

Among the first was Ben Bagdikian, in his RAND-funded *Information Machines*, from 1971. While certainly publisher-oriented and optimistic (to say the least) about the role of technology in improving the reach and ability of newspapers to do reporting, his basic belief in the role of networks and computers to democratize access to information was, if not prophetic, at least prescient.[13] He predicted, for example, the increasing importance of memory storage for journalism, and the ability to share and access it across platforms (what we might call "devices" today).[14] Bagdikian believed that the computer would be *the* central device for journalism by the end of the century, and he was right.

Another early, and underappreciated, observer of the initial computerization of the newsroom was British journalist-turned-scholar Anthony Smith. Because he was steeped deeply in the European experience of newsroom technology-adoption, writing as he was in the midst of change, his perspective remains useful.[15] *In situ*, Smith observed the rise of video-display terminals and centralized minicomputer systems, among other devices, which will be explored in more detail in this study. His insights, such as the challenges reporters would have in adapting to new means of inputting their stories, make his research still relevant today as a primary source.

In his words:

> The creation of editorial "front-end" systems (for reporters' direct input of text to the computer) depends entirely upon the acceptance by reporters of the use of vdt's [*sic*; video-display, or "dumb" terminals, otherwise abbreviated as VDTs] for normal work. Many older reporters preferred to retire rather than learn the new skills – which are greater than those necessary for typing.

He goes on: "The [VDT] had to pass from an outlandish and experimental tool to a glamorous modern necessity before front-end systems could be brought in to the average newspaper."[16] These and other observations from then-contemporary researchers have shaped my own study, along with this guiding question: *How did rank-and-file news workers, and their observers, experience the computerization of the newsroom as it happened? What does that mean for the present moment?*

Following Andrew Abbott, my focus therefore is on the actual *control* over work news workers felt they had, if not held in reality, during the latter Cold War,[17] with a focus not so much on tenuous and subjective attempts to pin down what, exactly, "professional" identities meant as affected by technology tools, but rather on what the situation was on the ground, in newsrooms and in the field.[18]

But as any study of digital-technology-wrought interregnums would be remiss without, I must mention the work of Elizabeth Eisenstein, and her research on the long and messy transition in Europe to printing technology from the handwritten processes (in the sixteenth century) that had come before.[19] Eisenstein, herself reacting to the ideas of Marshall McLuhan and his *Gutenberg Galaxy*, examined how printing did not arrive in one piece: many printers and many innovations had to occur, and not in a preordained way, for our book- (and ultimately magazine- and newspaper-) culture to take root.

Finally, though, among the studies most relevant to the transition to a more computerized, mobile newsroom during the 1970s and 1980s is the work of Matthew Kirschenbaum.[20] While he is more focused on the concepts underlying and embedded in "word processing" as it developed from the 1960s through the 1980s and the adoption of related software and hardware by elite authors, journalists-as-authors certainly benefited from the pioneering efforts of novelists and researchers alike (for instance: as will be explored in more depth, MIT collaborated with both writers and publishers in the 1970s to develop now-ubiquitous tools such as layout/pagination software, data transfer across networks and text editing). Kirschenbaum's call for specifics, in terms of programming, hardware manufacturers, donors, early users and so forth, has helped to drive this study in its quest for trends, dates, corporate research and development and other high-level trends in newsroom computerization.[21]

Following his admonition to pay attention to "very specific products and technologies" and "the particulars of different operating systems, software versions, and hardware protocols," wherever possible I have striven to include details about proprietary systems and thus specifics, and not generalities. Specific technologies lead to specific affordances.

It matters whether or not a device involved steps or new skill sets for news workers. These affordances are leveraged differently by different kinds of software and hardware in the newsroom. The "what" is not just an interesting digression, but matters because it mattered to the news workers who encountered transitory tools in their newsrooms during the 1960s through the 1990s, especially those centered around the computer. These places of work were not tabula rasa for early analog-digital techs, somehow appearing from nowhere and then changing everything; no, they had long, path-dependent histories of their own with technology, and came from somewhere and changed some things, gradually.[22]

Methods/sources

For this project I read and took notes on stories, photos and cartoons/illustrations in more than 400 issues of *Editor & Publisher*, more than 700 issues of *Columbia Journalism Review* and *Quill*, dozens of issues of *Newspaper Research Journal* and the ANPA's *News Research Bulletin*, and about contemporary, independent studies in book form from the era, along with archival material at the Living Computer Museum.[23] This is in addition to dozens of secondary sources, including the still-classic work of Martin Campbell-Kelly (examining the history of the American software industry) and Paul Ceruzzi (examining the history of computer hardware), along with more recent work by Claire Evans and Lisa Gitelman.[24] While not a history of the computer or of software, it was important to consult these works for context on the latter Cold War and early 1990s. The study's scope, as noted above, is limited to before the widespread adoption of the internet by American newspapers. That topic is worthy of a future study, and one that I would love to tackle with help from other scholars.

For further context, I consulted James Cortada's thorough bibliography of Cold War–era histories of computer integration/adoption.[25] Some of the material from the Living Computer Museum, it should be noted, especially on the System Integrators' Dakota VDT devices, along with other 1980s-era hardware and software related to word processing in the newspaper industry, has not been used before.

In addition, it should be acknowledged at the outset that the trade publications consulted come with their own inherent issues, primarily that of power and perspective. *Editor & Publisher*, in particular, along with the material from the American Newspaper Publishers Association (ANPA) and the American Society of News Editors (ASNE), was written from the point of view of owners and corporate bosses, not the rank-and-file and middle-management news workers on whom I am chiefly focused. That being said, however, the strategic overview of the industry provided by *Editor & Publisher* is helpful when deciphering the development and adoption of such expensive systems as computers.[26]

The pages of *Columbia Journalism Review* and *Quill*, published by Columbia's School of Journalism and the Society of Professional Journalists, respectively, provided a useful counterbalance to the influence of

Editor & Publisher, however, as their stories and commentaries were written by journalism educators, critics, working editors and reporters, and outsiders. The challenges of adopting to new work routines were a focus of these trade publications, but in more self-aware ways than has perhaps been appreciated. Particular attention was paid to accounts that dealt with discrepancies/disparities in power/access within the newsroom. I sought out diverse voices, including from women and people of color, whenever they appeared – in *Quill*, more often than not – but I also realize that these voices were often marginalized and silenced. I will seek to offer a partial corrective here, but that story deserves its own study.

It should be noted again that prior to this study there has not been an attempt to synthesize, even if briefly, a study of newsroom computerization and related technologies during the latter Cold War. Among other reasons for this, to my chagrin, I have discovered that the vast scope of such an undertaking would require years of dedicated time and effort. What follows then, as noted above, is simply a first attempt. But I believe that it helps to illuminate the challenges of predicting technology adoption, acceptance and rejection by news workers in our own time.

It might not be easy to predict what artificial intelligence and virtual reality might do in the near future to journalism, but media history shows that tech tools rarely lead directly to a clear, dark dystopia or an obvious, euphoric utopia. Reflecting the rest of reality, it is a bit of both.

News workers survived immense changes to their work environments long before the internet and the World Wide Web used to "browse" it arrived. Their resilience, their innovation and, more fundamentally, their voices will be highlighted wherever possible in this brief study. Following the examples of Bonnie Brennen and my other mentors, including Randy Beam, David Domke, Richard Kielbowicz, Doug Underwood and Betty Winfield, I hope to show that editors, reporters and other newsroom staff had ideas of their own, that they shaped their world and were not victims. If anything, newsroom technologies centered around the computer have a much longer, and more complex, history than perhaps has been previously appreciated. But more on that in a moment.

Overview of chapters/sections

Following this introduction, the second chapter will examine the first era of newsroom computerization in the form of mainframes and their attendant use as databases in large, daily newspapers, primarily on the East Coast, from the mid-1950s through the late 1960s, and the development of the first pagination software (by the ANPA's Research Institute), OCR tech and other relevant analog tools. Computers were used by large newspapers during the early Cold War, but their use as large-scale problem-solving machines (especially with circulation and payroll tasks) makes sense for the era.

The third chapter focuses on the "minicomputer" era, from *c.* 1970 through 1982, as the PDP-8 and VDTs, CRTs and other early "dumb terminals" and small local storage capabilities were beginning to transform larger newsrooms. This chapter reviews initial news-worker experiences with computers for editing and publication. It also covers the use of scanners and optical character recognition technology, and how these did not, in fact, become dominant.

The fourth chapter examines the microprocessor era, *c.* 1982–1992, and the rise of "smart" terminals, "microcomputers" and off-the-shelf hardware/ software, along with the increasing use of computers in smaller news organizations (including newspapers and radio/TV stations). The use of "personal computers" in newsrooms (particularly smaller newsrooms) and operating systems such as MS-DOS (Microsoft Disk Operating System), despite initial suspicion and cost, are reviewed.[27] The typical user/news-worker experience changed during this era with computers – these devices became more power, and therefore were more personalized, than ever before.

Chapter five covers the continued use of pre-internet networks, and wire services and bulletin boards deployed for user (i.e., reader) interaction. I – briefly – look at the integration of decentralized computer networks in newsrooms, with a mix of content-management systems and PCs, and the increasing use of pagers/cellphones for reporting/news-gathering, including the shift from "portable" to mobile conceptualizations for these technologies. Early efforts toward digital photography will also be reviewed.

Finally, in the conclusion, I briefly look at what happened in the mid-1990s and what came after, with the foreshadowing of the interactive Web 2.0, app-driven, mobile and generally more wired newsrooms of the twenty-first century, and review the limits of my research, along with future directions.

Notes

1 Here defined as journalists who worked in newsrooms on reporting and editing, but not necessarily commentators, editorial writers or columnists.

2 Here defined as the use of computers for newsroom work tasks by rank-and-file news workers, including editors and reporters, as contrasted to more elite users, such as publishers, owners or novelists (as studied ably by others).

3 Defined as the physical spaces, but in some cases also the distributed spaces, in which news workers did their jobs, and continue to do them.

4 Arguably, the generation of journalists emerging now, especially as virtual reality and other related technologies are still in their infancy, have experienced *less* technological change since *c.* 2010 than their mentors/predecessors did. The shift from analog to electric to "electronic" and then digital happened very quickly.

5 Matthew Kirschenbaum, *Track Changes: A Literary History of Word Processing* (Cambridge, MA: Harvard University Press, 2016). Kirschenbaum focuses on elite authors and their adoption of the word processor, such as Amy Tan, Stephen King and Isaac Asimov, along with some of the context for the development of word-processing software.

6 Pablo Boczkowski, "The Material Turn in the Study of Journalism: Some Hopeful and Cautionary Remarks from an Early Explorer," *Journalism* 16, no. 1 (2015): 65–68; Michael Schudson, "What Sorts of Things Are Thingy? And What Sorts of Thinginess Are There? Notes on Stuff and Social Construction," *Journalism* 16, no. 1 (2015): 61–64. I have tried to emulate their work in my own research, previously on early mobile-reporting technology for newsrooms; see Will Mari, "Technology in the Newsroom: Adoption of the Telephone and the Radio Car from *c.* 1920 to 1960," *Journalism Studies* 19, no. 9 (2018): 1366–1389.

7 Will Mari, *The American Newsroom: A Social History, 1920 to 1960* (Ph.D. dissertation, University of Washington, 2016).

8 As a careful reader of my citations will realize, I actually go a bit further in time, to *c.* 1992–1993, in order to cover the moment right before the internet was not only accessible to civilian researchers and entrepreneurs alike and fully and finally detached from the ARPANET and its successors, but also reachable and "surfable" via the World Wide Web and early browsers; "World Wide Web Timeline," Pew Research Center, Mar. 11, 2015, www.pewinternet.org/2014/03/11/world-wide-web-timeline/.

9 Matt Carlson, *Journalistic Authority: Legitimizing News in the Digital Era* (New York: Columbia University Press, 2017), 148–149, 161–162. Other influential scholars, such as Nikki Usher, C. W. Anderson, Matthew Powers, Seth Lewis and Silvio Waisbord, along with Pablo Boczkowski (and previously Barbie Zelizer, Michael Schudson and Randal Beam), have engaged with this topic in ways that are both helpful and far beyond the scope of this study.

10 Carlson, *Journalistic Authority*, 148–149.

11 Henrik Örnebring, "Technology and Journalism-as-Labor: Historical Perspectives," *Journalism* 11, no. 57 (2010); Nikki Usher, *Making News at the New York Times* (Ann Arbor, MI: University of Michigan Press, 2014); Mark Deuze, "What Is Journalism? Professional Identity and Ideology of Journalists Reconsidered," *Journalism* 6, no. 4 (2005): 442–464.

12 Kevin G. Barnhurst and John C. Nerone, *The Form of News: A History* (New York: Guilford Press, 2001), and Barbie Zelizer, *Taking Journalism Seriously: News and the Academy* (London: Sage, 2004).

13 Ben H. Bagdikian, *The Information Machines: Their Impact on Men and the Media* (New York: Harper & Row, 1971). While justly critiqued for being influenced by his corporate and government sponsors, Bagdikian was earnest and honest in ways that are underappreciated today.

14 Bagdikian, *The Information Machines*, 1971, 196–197.

15 Anthony Smith, *Goodbye Gutenberg: The Newspaper Revolution of the 1980s* (New York: Oxford University Press, 1980).

16 Smith, *Goodbye Gutenberg*, 1980, 97.

17 Here defined as the post-Vietnam era, during the first and more sustained efforts at "thawing" the extended geopolitical standoff between East and West. Note, however, that I am not a Cold War historian nor do I want to pretend to be: this is simply the broader historical context for this study. For a far more insightful

take on what Cold War-era politics and technologies meant for the computer industry under the control of the Warsaw Pact and its controlling power, the Soviet Union and its empire, I would defer to Ben Peters and his recent and seminal work on the Soviet internet, *How Not to Network a Nation* (Cambridge, MA: MIT Press, 2017).

18 Andrew Abbott, *The System of Professions* (Chicago: University of Chicago Press, 1988).

19 Elizabeth Eisenstein, *The Printing Revolution in Early Modern Europe* (Cambridge: University of Cambridge Press, 2005, Second Edition). It should be noted that this is a condensed version of Eisenstein's longer work, *The Printing Press as an Agent of Change*, published in 1979 and still critical when considering the history of the book.

20 Kirschenbaum, *Track Changes.*

21 Kirschenbaum, *Track Changes*, 13, 14–15, 24–25, 37. Again, while focused on the imagination caught up in, and integral to, word processing, Kirschenbaum's intensely *material* analysis of literary conceptions of technology and writing was and remains very important to my work on news workers and reporting tools/technologies. Tools can be both affordances and also represent larger ideas of independence, professionalization and even "work." There is no need for a bifurcated approach.

22 Kirschenbaum, *Track Changes*, 26–27; for important theoretical work, see Jennifer Earl and Katrina Kimport, *Digitally Enabled Social Change: Activism in the Internet Age* (Cambridge, MA: MIT Press, 2011).

23 Wherever possible, because I had access to complete runs of material from *c.* 1965 onward, I generally used a representative sampling for the higher-frequency (i.e., weekly) publications such as *Editor & Publisher* (for the years *c.* 1957–1960, and *c.* 1977–1983, a moment of markedly intense transition from very little computer use to some use, and then proprietary to more ersatz, or centralized to more decentralized systems, respectively, I read approximately every other issue of *E&P*, along with every special June tech issue and its successor, recap issue, but for the years 1970–1976, and *c.* 1984–1992, I read one issue a month, using a progressive, representative sampling method, i.e., the first, second, third, fourth and fifth issues, as applicable, for each month throughout the year, while still reading the June tech issues or any other special tech, i.e., "the PC issue" from Sept. 1988, as observed). For lower-frequency publications, such as *Columbia Journalism Review* and *Quill* (which usually came out monthly), I read every issue that could be located. For the *Newspaper Research Journal* and the *Bulletins*, I consulted relevant indexes, with a special focus on the era from *c.* 1984–1992. Two examples of contemporary accounts of newsroom computerization, in addition to those noted later, are Paul Williams, *The Computerized Newspaper: A Practical Guide for Systems Users* (Oxford: Heinemann Professional Publishing, Ltd., 1990) and Nancy Carter and John Cullen, *Computerization of Newspaper Organizations: The Impact of Technology on Organizational Structuring* (Lanham, MD: University Press of America, 1983). A reasonable attempt, with the restrictions brought on by other projects and deadlines, was made to find material that provided insight into the computerization of the newsroom during the era in question. Further details of representative sampling methods will be provided in the research notes in the main body of the study, or in the bibliography.

24 Martin Campbell-Kelly, *From Airline Reservations to Sonic the Hedgehog: A History of the Software Industry* (Cambridge, MA: MIT Press, 2003), Paul Ceruzzi, *A History of Modern Computing* (Cambridge, MA: MIT Press, 2003); Claire L. Evans, *Broad Band: The Untold Story of the Women Who Made the Internet* (New York: Penguin, Random House, 2018); Lisa Gitelman, *Paper Knowledge: Toward a Media History of Documents* (Durham, NC: Duke University Press, 2014).

25 James W. Cortada, *A Bibliographic Guide to the History of Computing, Computers, and the Information Processing Industry* (New York: Greenwood Press, 1990). See also James W. Cortada, *A Bibliographic Guide to the History of Computer Applications, 1950–1990* (Westport, CT: Greenwood Press, 1996).

26 Generally, I will attempt to specify whether or not I am talking about larger minicomputers versus, say, microprocessors, which come later on in the story of newsroom computerization. While I am not a programmer or a computer engineer, I have consulted with both kinds of individuals when faced with a challenging term or technical description I did not understand.

27 Such as the TRS-80, other IBM clones and Apple IIe then SE and variants.

2   The mainframe era

Initial computerization of the newsroom from the mid-1950s to the 1960s

Well over a generation before the internet arrived in all its commercial and creative force on the American journalism scene in the 1990s, there were computers in newsrooms. Beginning in at least the mid-1950s, in fact, mainframe computers were finding their way into an elite few news organizations on the East Coast for large-scale, niche problems, such as organizing subscriber information or deciphering payroll.

These early efforts were, however, not part of a trend toward newsroom computerization per se. Newspapers were still factories in the 1950s and 1960s. Information was turned into a daily or weekly paper product through mechanical steps that were many, varied and expensive. In the words of one news worker who entered the industry in 1967 as an "editorial trainee" (essentially an intern):

> It was an overwhelmingly analog and artisanal process, born of great machines, hot metal, and great skill – not to mention thousands upon thousands of words and hundreds on hundreds of photographs. The two groups that put all this together – the craft people and the editorial people – worked together harmoniously for the most part, provided one did not invade the other's turf, most notably in the composing room.[1]

It was not until the late 1960s, and the creation of an informal and then formal alliance between MIT and the American Newspaper Publishers Association (ANPA) Research Institute, the latter based in Easton, Pennsylvania, that news organizations began to think seriously about using computers to solve more than a handful of specialized problems. As a result, ultimately, that harmony between the editorial and production sides of the news factories would fade away, not due to animosity, but to the reality that editorial workers would take on more and more production-related tasks.

MIT's brand and brains lent legitimacy to what had been a much more industrially focused operation, examining processes relevant to production and less so the editorial side of the newspaper business. But with the development of prototype layout software for the PDP-8 and related research on programming for optical character recognition (OCR) and other word-processing techniques, the ANPA's Research Institute began to split its focus by the early 1970s and its relocation to Easton, Pennsylvania. Its small team of programmers pioneered the use of the computer for the newsroom for tasks that went beyond the use of mainframes and instead found numerous uses for the generation of minicomputers that would become the heart of first-generation newsroom pagination systems.

These systems were centralized, and involved "dumb" video-display terminals (VDTs) used by a fraction of the newsroom staff and supervised by editors who also typically had to share access to various new input devices. Some of the early set-ups involved OCR scanning, but eventually most used direct inputs via keyboards (and in some early cases, light pens, for layout).

As microprocessors became more affordable in the early 1980s, more decentralized systems appeared. These "personal computer" (PC) oriented systems were first considered less capable than the proprietary machines that had come before (with their limited local memory and graphical abilities). But a number of factors led to the general acceptance outside of newsrooms of computers-as-office-work tools for the individual, versus the collective: these included the advent of faster IBM and Macintosh devices, the use of UNIX and other networking software, the introduction of first-generation word-processing software and operating systems that did not need sophisticated programming ability. In time, these off-the-shelf, more ersatz systems became the norm.

It was much more common for a news worker at the end of the 1980s and the start of the 1990s, immediately prior in the latter case to the introduction of civilians having their own computer, or at least only having to share it with a few others.

Within the newsroom, then, the great shift in computerization, from a rarity used by only the largest and most daringly innovative, to the prosaic and diffused, happened within a generation and at a rate of adoption that rivaled and exceeded that of cars, telephones or even typewriters.

Granted, there were limitations to newspaper and newsroom computerization – many processes, especially on the production side, remained relatively untouched by computer control and interaction well into the 1990s. But a wide variety of activities, including everything from information-searching in databases to payroll, circulation, classified ad-taking and of course word processing and editing, were increasingly computerized by the mid-1980s. The *Chicago Tribune*, for example, in September 1986 stopped taking unsolicited manuscripts that had to be typed up (or in the lingo of the era, "keyboarded into") for their "electronic editing and typesetting systems" and would only take them on IBM-compatible disks.[2] This marked a definite shift from an earlier era, when only copy that had been typed on a Selectric or other electric typewriter would be considered legitimate.[3]

How computers first appeared in newsrooms: enter the mainframes

Beyond exceptions that included the world of elite authors, parts of law, medicine and government, though, the newspaper industry and its workers in the decades from the 1950s through the end of the century, but especially the 1970s and 1980s, were among the first to adopt computers whole-scale and to weave them into daily work rhythms in indispensable ways. Partially because of the sheer volume of wire-service copy, along with local content, newspapers and their staffs were keen to use whatever technological tools – despite initial anxiety and trepidation in many cases – to gather/collect, organize and publish information. As part of the early information economy, journalism in the United States (and also in the UK, Western Europe and Canada, along with Japan, Mexico and a few other centers of journalistic innovation that are outside the scope of this project) was caught up in the larger software and hardware revolution of the latter Cold War but also helped to drive it. Reporters and editors were the ideal consumers of white-collar-workplace computer-based tools. Without their influence and need for these tools, one could argue that many of the devices and programs we take for granted, even those fairly esoteric-for-the-time (and still fairly new for ours) tools such as voice-activated software (eventually leading to the semantic web), had, if not their origin, then a strong kick toward that end, in newsroom needs. While some scholars have argued convincingly that this has come at the expense of news workers' agency, these same workers believed that computers could solve previously expensive or even insoluble issues.[4]

The internet and the Web would only drive the pace of innovation forward faster. The groundwork had been set in the period of turmoil and change (though still within the context of fairly healthy profit margins) for news-media organizations and companies that was the 1970s and 1980s. But looking at the impact of the internet on the newsroom in the 1990s and 2000s, through and then after Web 2.0, is worth its own sustained study. Here we will concern ourselves with how the computer changed things, and how news workers changed the computer.

It would be a long time before a typical news worker would see a computer in her or his newsroom. In fact, it would be a while before one could find a computer at all in any newsroom anywhere. But computers – represented by VDTs made by manufacturers such as Hendrix, Harris and Raytheon – would appear in newsrooms in force by the mid-1970s. What happened in the meantime?

Authors writing retrospectives at the end of the 1980s reflected on how gradual the shift to the ubiquitous VDT had occurred, even at mid-sized (50,0000- to 100,000-daily circulation) or smaller newspapers. Typing on a screen – something that as recently as the mid-1960s felt like it belonged in the realm of science fiction – was the everyday normal. The arrival of "smart" terminals seemed like the next logical step.

But the jump from a computer-less to a computerized newsroom (and not just with word processors, but also with access to databases/early networks, digital photography and design) had not been preordained.

The ANPA and MIT

The origins of the American Newspaper Publishers Association (ANPA) Research Institute could be traced to 1954 and the rise of television as a rival to newspapers. Among other projects, the Institute sponsored efforts to improve "cold" printing and page makeup, as well as related offset printing technologies, and developed improvements aimed at extending the life of "hot" printing machines (that recast metal type with each daily printing run).[5] Industry executives fretted about the price of paper, the (slight) drop-off in revenue due to the presence of broadcast news and the cost of maintaining their news factories. Partially to allay such fears, the Institute sponsored annual production-oriented conferences, usually held in early June, and invited manufacturers to demonstrate equipment and network. The Institute also produced the ANPA *Research Bulletin* and generally promoted close collaboration between vendors and newspaper owners. *Editor & Publisher*, as the unofficial voice of the industry, was an enthusiastic cheerleader for its efforts, and ran ads for everything from paper-storage systems to Linotypes. These ran alongside positive reviews and enthusiastic essays on the potential for new manufacturing and methods to save money and ensure newspapers' survival in the era of color TV.

A few large newspapers, including the *New York World Telegram and Sun* and the *Philadelphia Inquirer*, experimented with using mainframe computers in the 1950s and 1960s. The former used a Remington Rand Univac 60 Punched-Card Electronic Computer to decipher the complex payroll schedules, pay scales and nuances of contracts of its ten labor unions and 1,800 employees. It took five hours to prepare the computer for its uniquely designed programs, and "a few hours of automatic processing." But what had taken days now took hours.[6] There were also early experiments with phototypesetting during this decade, some of which led to more advanced electro-mechanical hybrid devices that, while not run by computers, set the stage for future adaption to them.[7]

In 1954, a memo by David Podvey, the business manager of the *Philadelphia Inquirer*, describes a project that involved renting an IBM mainframe and creating a punch-card device that could monitor ad production. IBM insisted on a legal waiver that would release their company from any blame if the idea did not work out. But using an IBM punch-card system speeded up the process of finding revenue information on ads, from days to minutes, and ultimately led the *Inquirer* to try out other early techniques involving computers, including an early example of a story based on a software program's analysis of databases. Other early efforts in this vein included the work of IBM's Hans Peter Luhn, who "produced an automatic document-indexing program" in 1958, and that would later help start the computer-assisted journalism movement, which arguably began with Philip Meyer's study of African Americans affected by the 1967 Detroit riots, and, in turn, ultimately helped the *Detroit Free Press* win a Pulitzer Prize.[8]

But by the early 1960s, some members of the Institute were interested in using computers to do some of the work of production, and even ease the burden on newsroom staff, who typically did not concern themselves with the industrial-plant part of the newspaper until they reached senior management, and even then, only minimally. The International Typographical Union (ITU) ran their closed and powerful "shops" (or union chapters) at most newspapers without competition, and were present at even supposedly non-unionized papers. Their highly paid and experienced workers (earning hundreds of dollars a week when reporters, for example, made a third or less) controlled the many steps needed to get a piece of typewritten paper produced on newsprint.

Richard Steele, the director of the ANPA Research Institute, encouraged his staff to collaborate with the Massachusetts Institute of Technology on the latter's Information Transfer Experiments (or INTREX) project, with the blessing of the ANPA's Scientific Advisory Committee, on basic research, particularly pertaining to the computerization of newsroom work processes.[9] Steele, the former publisher of the *Worcester Telegram & Evening Gazette*, was aware of the challenge in wedding the conservative newspaper industry to MIT's experimental work.

But by 1966, the ANPA was funding research by J. Francis Reintjes, director of MIT's Electronic Systems Laboratory, on "Project INTREX." While a major focus for the project under Reintjes was information management for university libraries and networks, the goal with newspapers was to find ways of "storing and retrieving news articles in an on-line [*sic*], time-sharing computer environment," which made sense in an era where even a single mainframe could cost a corporation $100,000.[10] Among other objectives, ANPA wanted relevant research on the following objectives, including:

1 Inputting of full text of news articles into the computer from the Teletypesetter tapes regularly used in newspaper typesetting operations.
2 Automatic indexing of the subject content of these articles.
3 Rapid retrieval of these articles, or references to them, through on-line, interactive user-computer dialogue at consoles remote from the [central] computer.
4 In-depth manual cataloging of these same articles for purposes of comparing the utility of automatic and human indexing.[11]

Not all of these subprojects panned out as expected.[12] But what did emerge was – eventually – revolutionary, allowing publishers to undercut the power of production workers and shift control of newspaper operations more completely to the newsroom.

As Steele put it, while uncertain as to the ultimate direction of the research, "eventually, these pieces of hardware and software will be molded into a total newspaper system." He cautioned, however, that people would be intrinsic to any use of computers and that they would not be replaced wholesale by even the more ambitious technologies envisioned at the time by MIT and ANPA researchers.

"Today the editor is limited in scope because of the pressure of time and mechanical restrictions. Tomorrow many of these restraints will be lifted and he will fully be able to offer his unique contribution to his newspaper and his readers."[13]

More immediately, a "story monitoring and viewing program," with cathode-ray tube (CRT) displays, a "story editing system" also on CRTs and allowing for corrections, and a "page-layout and 'dummying' technique program" with the ability to use the CRT displays to prototype what would be later printed were among the immediate results of the ANPA-MIT collaboration.

The first three projects would more or less appear as video-display terminals (VDTs, which were less bulky and built specifically for use by news workers), especially those sold by Hendrix, and memory in minicomputers, along with word processing software and hardware, in the mid- to late-1970s.[14] The last would show up in the layout-software written for the PDP-8 minicomputer, which would become an early workhorse for newsroom computerization efforts.[15]

As early as June 1970, an editorial in *Editor & Publisher* declared that "science has invaded the newsroom and with it the scientific brains from the production department," so much so that the "editor of the future will have an engineering degree as well as a journalism degree in order to know how to operate his newsroom full of computers and CRTs."[16] One year later, Steele wrote that the Institute would help "to get the 'lead out' of this area of newspaper machinery operations," and somewhat optimistically added that "the video tube is rapidly becoming an integral part of composing rooms in newspapers, both offset and letterpress, throughout the country."

Early software programs for newsroom computing

But the practical way these prognostications became reality was through the hard work of a handful of ANPA RI staffers.

These included Dave Reed, research manager for computer applications, Bill Rinehart, vice president, Erwin Jaffe, director of research, and Richard Cichelli, another staff researcher. Many of their projects with MIT focused on newspaper layout, and it was Rinehart who advocated for the adoption of minicomputers, specifically the various models developed by Digital Equipment Corporation (DEC), and in particular the PDP-8 series, for use in newsrooms, toward that end. Jaffe focused on "building a portable reporter terminal," and lobbied publishers to consider using/buying the tech, as well as manufacturers such as Teleram, though that would take some time.

Reed developed early grammar-analysis programs that would recommend trimming excess words, using "statistical measures to rate the relevance of paragraphs and sentences within a story." Other early programs developed in the late 1960s and early 1970s included CLASS, or the Classified Ad Storage and Sorting Program, for layout of ads using an IBM 1130 computer, and available to any ANPA-member paper at a reduced cost. Grammar-analysis programs and CLASS were "entirely new products [built] to help overcome several serious bottlenecks in our newspapers' production and distribution systems," Steele recalled later.[17]

But it was the "page dummying" work of Reed that had the most immediate impact on the industry.

Previously, "pages," or newspaper layouts, had been pasted up, or arranged, by hand, to be photographed and made into plates. Reed had the idea that software could at least expedite the process, which was time-consuming, and meant that late-breaking copy – the kind designed to compete with TV and radio news – could be added later and more accurately.

In a pilot project, an original layout program, Layout-8, the programming for which Reed was largely responsible, was installed at the Marion, Indiana, *Chronicle-Tribune*. The ANPA *Research Bulletin* helped to spread the word about the program, and, according to Cichelli and a 1986 account, "So many newspapers wanted copies of the program that just punching the cards and shipping them all over the country would have constituted a significant budget item for the fledgling ANPA RI computer applications department." The institute decided to charge $30 for the program, which could run on an IBM 1130 with just 8 kilobytes of memory.[18]

A successor program, used in pagination (or connected, laid-out pages), became a major focus for the RI in 1973; written in FORTRAN, it was just 6,000 lines long. This program, in turn, was succeeded by Layout-80, and installed by the early 1980s on about 40 newspapers. In either case, a big early hurdle was processing power, but bigger/faster minicomputers overcame this by about 1975, which Cichelli identifies as a key "transition point. That was the year I felt you could buy a newspaper front-end system with the reasonable expectation that it would actually work just as the vendor said it would." It is notable that all this pioneering work was done by essentially three staff members, but that original team expanded and went on to work on tertiary projects, including a dedicated spell checker.[19]

Manufacturers such as Hendrix, Harris and dozens of others followed suit, building and selling proprietary programs that could be purchased wholesale by publishers, who were keen to minimize disruption. Not out of concern for news workers, per se – they desired, instead, to maximize profits and marginalize the power of unions. However, the ANPA's Research Institute was not the only place where experimentation with computing was taking place in the 1960s and early 1970s. Some enterprising newsrooms had already started.

OCR technology as a path only partially taken

Optical character recognition (OCR) was a bridge technology between analog input and later, digitally manipulated and designed, text-editing methods. An early OCR reader, such as that by the aptly named Character Recognition Machine (CRM) Corp., priced at a "relatively low $89,000" in 1970 (or $588,000 in 2018 dollars), and while still partially experimental, was designed to be used with an early CRT display, a PDP-8-L minicomputer, an ASR-334 Teletype console keyboard, and a "high-speed Teletype-Burpee tape punch."[20] The whole system was built to have an "on-line editing function," which meant it could be used in real-time with other production processes and devices. CRM claimed it could replace up to 12–15 people; however, it was a fairly intensive machine to use, with up to 500 words per minute of input via its OCR scanner, but requiring specialized training to operate.[21]

OCR was thought of as a minimally disruptive way to get typed copy from reporters, via editors, to terminals for editing (usually via paper tape, for input and output) and then on to typesetting and printing. Numerous examples from trade publications attest to this belief, and the resulting sea change when "paperless" systems began to appear in the mid-1970s. Many smaller publishers preferred the cheaper, if less-robust, OCR method of text-input through the mid-1970s.

OCR was not "just" a stepping stone. Less revolutionary than evolutionary, news workers (and especially editors) valued it in its own right, because it allowed copy to be typeset with fewer errors and faster than human proofreaders could check. It also let copy flow right up to press time (though it didn't yet have the same "on-line" capacity of "paperless" VDTs). Early stories emphasized the reduction in the error rates found in news copy. Sloppy work could and did occur – because early OCRs needed some special coding to work, and reporters would sometimes not bother with retyping.

In 1971, at a newspaper production conference in Chicago, a proof-of-concept direct-input terminal system was built in a marathon series of meetings over about 100 hours. Using several Harris 1100 VDTs, a Hendrix 3400 minicomputer and Associated Press (AP) wire stories for content, along with a Compgraphic 4961 typesetter, the feasibility, at least in small batches, of putting copy directly on a digital "page" and then producing them as special tabloids was demonstrated. This allowed the conference organizers to bypass other, more cumbersome input methods, such as typing up copy on electric typewriters, scanning them via OCR, and having to collect the wire copy on paper tape (which had previously been allowed to spool upon arrival in a garbage can).[22]

Early experiments like this have plenty of limitations, including the fact that OCR-scanned copy still had to be used, and that, in turn, involved the use of customized paper and the use of alphanumeric codes to speed the input process. Such was the lingering problem of errors creeping into the scanning process that software was later built, in some cases, to detect and fix this later phenomenon.[23]

As one journalist-turned-innovator explained, "OCR technology was little used and only for demonstration. VDTs were far more popular with the staff of 'young kids,' mostly interns. It was like a new toy to them. Our problem was pulling them off the chair so we could get someone else writing copy."[24] Despite their lack of glamour, OCRs helped to drive the adoption of computers at daily and weekly newspapers of all sizes and circulations. And while editors and publishers, eager to prove their risky, and pricey, investment of such technology was worth it, downplayed resistance from news workers (especially from reporters), some of the latter did indeed dislike the new gear.

Tom Eblen, a "veteran reporter" turned city editor at the *Kansas City Star*, wrote a tongue-in-cheek poem about this pushback in 1973, as his paper started adopting OCR-based work processes:

> To hell with the electric typewriter machine.
> To hell with the cathode tubes.
> They'll slow down production, cause morale reduction.
> And turn us into blithering boobs.
> Hurray for my battered Underwood.
> Hurray for my trusted Royal.
> Hurray [*sic*] for those wonder white pencils
> And all the other artifacts with which we toil.
> Modernization? We shun it.
> We wanta [*sic*] do it like we always done it.[25]

By the summer of 1974, however, using two Compuscan 170 minicomputers, the newspaper was in the process of fully switching to OCR, in cooperation with the ANPA RI, with Selectrics used to reduce errors. Most of the reporters at the paper adapted to the new processes, and although writing for OCR scanning involved allowing very few mistakes and could be challenging for rookie typists, exposure and practice with any hybrid OCR system seemed to help smooth over ruffled egos.[26]

OCR was popular with publishers as well because it allowed their editorial staff members to get used to computers, and it delayed the more totalizing change later brought on by word processors (and before that, VDT-based text-input systems). As one industry analyst put it, "The change for reporters may be as relatively minor as substituting new IBM electric typewriters [Selectrics] for old Underwood manuals."[27]

That same year, an OCR device used at the *Worcester Telegram & Evening Gazette*, itself a test bed for new journalism technology, also came with an $89,000 price tag, and took up to four to six months to get delivered. The optical scanner was described as "a hard-copy to paper or magnetic tape, converter," that read characters and then inputted text to tape, that was fed to a typesetting minicomputer and then a phototypesetter or linecasting machine.[28] Part of their expense was the need for a corresponding purchase of minicomputers, such as the popular PDP-8 series.[29] But the corresponding need for updating typewriters, investing in "cold-type" technology (often part of the impetus to reduce production-associated labor costs) and renovating aging newspaper buildings meant that larger costs were associated with new equipment.[30] OCR technology promised to maximize limited resources.[31]

Designed to be used with IBM Courier 12 font, produced by IBM Selectric typewriters that cost $480 each, or a modified Royal typewriter that cost $335, one such device was fed by an 8 1/8 x 11-inch input bay, with each triple-spaced page being read at a rate of 20 seconds per page, or 600–800 characters a minute, and designed to reduce the "bottleneck" of manual input.

Errors in text prepared by these devices could supposedly run as low as five per 10,000 characters. A VDT display was sometimes used to correct copy that contained errors, which helped to reduce that error rate even further. An operator would still need to mark special, OCR-readable codes in order to update copy; some of these could be done by hand with a pencil, but others needed a typewriter. In theory up to 500 ads could be handled in an hour with the computer and reader and one operator, versus the 3.5 hours required before with six TTS operators.[32]

One sticking point for these devices was in fact the marks, but also the typewriter-provided copy. Small errors could creep back in the process. Some typewriters did not work well with some OCR scanners, while others did. The *Army Times* had a rocky transition to partial OCR adoption in 1973, having to use IBM Selectric II typewriters instead of those built by Olivetti. The specific font (in this case, again the Courier 12) was challenging to scan.[33] Another continued point of conflict centered on training. While not as stark a jump as the leap from typewriters to terminals, reporters would balk at not being consulted before management switched wholesale to OCR-read copy, and needed to be brought into the acquisition process early if their use was to go smoothly.[34] OCR tech would coexist alongside VDT, if only because it was, ultimately, cheaper to use once newsrooms became more computerized.[35]

As Mike Lindsey, the publisher of the *Lewistown Sentinel* in Pennsylvania, explained, he did not want his reporters to be "secretaries, nor have them remember a lot of codes . . . that's why we choose terminals and not OCR," ultimately.[36] While worker satisfaction was not necessarily high on many other publisher's lists of priorities (cost saving was far more important), and such language reveals deeper concepts of gendered labor, being able to creatively engage your news workers did pay off in the sense that one's workers found their tasks more interesting and independent and they thus tended to be more effective and long-lasting in their jobs.

What newsroom computerization looked like in the early 1970s

In 1971, journalist and researcher Ben Bagdikian's book on the technology of the newsroom (or rather, the future of that technology) was published by the RAND Corporation, a unique government-nonprofit hybrid organization. One of their tasks was to produce research on the early information economy, especially work that pertained to military-industrial projects.[37] *The Information Machines: Their Impact on Men and the Media*, following in that vein, was ambitious in scope, pro-publisher and focused overwhelmingly on the positive impact of technology, including computers, on news organizations.[38] But despite his study's title, Bagdikian was fascinated by more than machines.

While not trained as a sociologist, Bagdikian was interested in how news workers operated within their organizations, influenced by Warren Breed's classic study on newsrooms as well as his own experiences in journalism.[39]

Observing that journalists were increasingly professionalized and educated, he believed that this meant they could be both more receptive to, and better at adopting, computer technology in their daily jobs.[40] Citing the pioneering work of J.C.R. Licklider, he believed that news workers were already at the forefront of changes in how information was gathered, stored and disseminated.[41] The solution to an increasingly overwhelming media ecosystem was access to information via digital means, Bagdikian believed. As he put it, "The American public is about to have the electronic computer enter their lives as a mechanism for social change as widespread as the automobile and television set."[42]

Most newspaper readers, he predicted, would consume their news at home via hybrid analog-digital devices, would assume that editors and reporters would act as researchers as well as storytellers and expected their news to be more curated, more customized and more immediate (as well as more analytical – a tall combined order indeed).[43]

But Bagdikian also believed that one danger of this more fragmented, more selective news experience – so different than that provided by the major networks of his era – was the presence of "racist interpretations" of, for instance, a Supreme Court decision. Ultimately, though, having computer networks provide the content of news organizations would result in a better, more healthy body politic, he thought, despite the risks. Writing as he was during the waning years of Vietnam, the Nixon presidency and the general societal and cultural upheaval of his era, Bagdikian was nothing if not optimistic.[44]

Imperfect prophet as he was, Bagdikian was on to something profound. Though not the only one to believe that news and computer networks should work together (military researchers working on the Advanced Research Projects Agency Network being another set of thinkers, along with others), he was among the first to describe, even if in vague terms, how important it was for journalistic organizations to adopt, and even pioneer, information processing and dissemination via computers.

To get there, practically, newsrooms would need to computerize, and quickly, using off-the-shelf technology. Bagdikian describes how computers were already helping to hyphenate (and justify, sometimes referred to as "H&J") text, tracing this process back to the introduction of the teletypesetter in the early 1930s and the use of perforated tape – and well before that, with the use of Linotype machines beginning in the 1890s.

By 1960 (so just over a decade before Bagdikian's study), computers were able to do some of the work of pagination, as the newspaper industry shifted to offset, "cold type" processes driven by photographic-capture methods (some involving early analog-digital scanning), part of the "linkage of computers and photocomposition" that would take a generation but ultimately move newspapers away from more industrial to more nimble production methods.[45]

Bagdikian describes a parallel pressure, that of processing wire copy. From the Associated Press alone (among several others), one teletype machine received messages composed of news briefs throughout the day in a newsroom, to the tune of nearly 30,000 words. Some larger newspapers had a dozen or more of these machines, and their overwhelmed news staff could never hope to skim and use more than a fraction of the news they were receiving (no more than about 20 percent, he estimated). On a large daily newspaper, then, factoring in local news content, about 110,000 words, or a good-sized book, had to be processed and produced in a 24-hour news cycle, at a minimum.[46]

The solution to this flood of information would be indexed copy controlled by computer processes, including digital displays (what Bagdikian called "video screen console[s]"), edited and written by news workers in real time, "simultaneously" working together on updating and altering stories as needed. In the vernacular of that moment, these systems would be "online," as noted earlier with OCR technology.[47] At a moment when computers were still thought of as single-problem (or at most a few-problem) solving devices, this was a fairly revolutionary rethinking of their role in newsrooms. Bagdikian also imagined images being edited in this way. This "digital darkroom" concept, as it came to be known, will be explored later in the study, as developed by a partnership between the Associated Press, MIT and the ANPA, and with a rival system created by United Press International (UPI).

On the reader's side, the printed form would endure for a generation or so or more, but eventually, the news would "much later, [be] transmitted electronically" on "the consumer's home console," changing the role of journalistic gatekeepers and passing some of that responsibility to the news consumers themselves.[48]

Bagdikian was clear about his allegiance to government-corporate interests, at least for the duration of his RAND research on the newspaper industry. In later, follow-up reflections, including in a *Columbia Journalism Review* article from 1973, he continued to express his belief that computers would be critical partners with the news-gathering, editing and publishing processes that had been so dominated for so long by artisanal and, later, industrial methods: "Without most working journalists knowing it, the . . . old fifteenth-century factories they work in are finally starting the terrifying leap from typewriter and lead pot to cathode ray tube and computer."[49]

Bagdikian credited the customization and use of existing tech, but also the development of newsroom-specific tools by the AP and UPI, for this soon-to-come rapid change. Declining prices on hardware also helped. He noted that the average price for CRTs (which he defined as "TV-like screens with keyboards connected to computers") had fallen dramatically, from $80,000 a piece in 1969 to $5,000 to $18,000 in early 1973.

Optical scanners, "computers that read carefully typed copy" had gone down from a peak price of $90,000 in 1970 to $60,000 in 1973; and the cost of "computer time" (or access to computers if you did not own them yourself) had gone from $200,000 in 1955 to as little as a dollar an hour. In 1963 he claimed that only 1 percent of American daily newspapers used computers; by 1973 some 60 percent did.[50,51]

At the *Detroit News*, one of the most automated papers outside of the wire services, 48 CRTs and 12 more ordered meant that up to 30 to 40 percent of all copy at the paper, including AP and UPI wire stories along with local stories, were "handled electronically without conventional typing or editing with paper and pencil."[52] The paper used a Hendrix 5700, with a screen that showed 18 lines of copy in 22-point type; a reporter could "slug" (i.e., title) a story and use simple letter combinations, including "LO" for local stories and "SP" for sports, the letters of his/her last name, and the slug proper (any six letters to describe the story) before selecting which edition the story was for, as well as the date.[53] Editing in real time in this way allowed copy to be placed within ten minutes of its being written on a CRT display, so that copy could be sent in late, adding hours of margin to assignments.

Computerized newsroom technologies had gone from looking like "badly managed paper recycling plants, with endless rolls of teletype snaking around machines, and desks piled high . . . banks of clattering teletype machines sounded like the shuttle room of a Woonsocket textile mill" by the end of 1973 to far quieter, more efficient spaces, especially at the more centralized UPI headquarters in NYC:

> The only sound is a soft squirting noise from about sixty Extel printers typing abstracts of stories being stored in the computers downstairs; the sound is inaudible from three feet away because the sixty-word-a-minute machines imprint by delicate letter- and number-shaped perforation[s] of paper whose interior is purple, producing purple letters. Only occasionally is there the noise of a typewriter or the nostalgic sound of two remaining teletypes.[54]

The UPI office alone in 1973 was managing an input of some three million words a day, with some 80 percent being sent out with help from early CRT displays, which led to fewer typos and transmission errors. The point, though, was not fewer mistakes. It was better information management: "These same digital impulses that carry news stories can, if publishers standardize . . . practically eliminate the major part of their newspaper factories – the composing room, stereotyping, photocomposition set-ups for offset, and conventional plate-making."[55]

With the wire services' early computerization efforts, Bagdikian noted the different organizing schema for the UPI and the AP, with the former having one central headquarters, using three RCA Spectra 70/45 computers to store all of its national and most of its international news; 34 VDTs had replaced 90 teletype machines; the VDTs were used with Harris-Intertype 1100s; five terminals in Washington, D.C., and three in Chicago were used to process broadcast wire.

Bureaus and correspondents still filed by teletype, but the copy went directly into the system's computers. From the outset, though, the AP had a much more distributed system, with ten regional HQs, along with 38 bureaus and 75 field offices; all had terminals that could send copy, and also used "datafax," a fax machine from which copy would be retyped directly into a terminal.[56]

The AP's NYC office had one small computer and 25 VDTs, also built by Hendrix, and costing $14,000 each, compared to the UPI's Harris models, which cost $18,000, but which were a bit easier to learn how to use. Other smaller differences: the AP's display was black with white letters and used a flashing white cursor, and it had more command keys, some with triple functions.[57]

Bagdikian observed that the wire services had an advantage with early conversion to CRT/VDT displays in that they were focused on news/journalism-gathering and editing and not publication, per se. Optimistically, he noted that there had been "no massive resistance to the new machines," including in the first location the AP deployed their VDTs, at its Columbia, South Carolina, bureau; he quotes Wes Gallagher, the AP's chief, who claimed that "everyone liked and accepted the new system, including the older men."

He similarly glowingly reported on how early VDTs were faring at the UPI's more centralized system. Letting reporters and editors "play" with the machines at the UPI's office and "make mistakes . . . privately" seemed to help with their acceptance. William Laffler, a veteran UPI staff member who had been with the organization for 28 years, said that he had been

> skeptical at first but I found things easier. The screen is always clear and even. Before, when reporters did rewrite, some had clean copy, some had dirty copy; some had black ribbons, and some had faded ones; and when you read all day it's annoying. Also, I can see what I've got in one glance.[58]

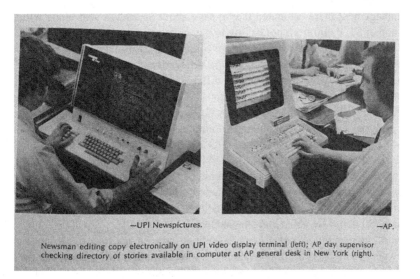

—UPI Newspictures.   —AP.

Newsman editing copy electronically on UPI video display terminal (left); AP day supervisor checking directory of stories available in computer at AP general desk in New York (right).

Figure 2.1   Ben Bagdikian, "Publishing's Quiet Revolution," *Columbia Journalism Review*, May/June 1973.

Bagdikian noted that "wire service executives appeared so euphoric about acceptance of the new machines that it seemed wise to check with representatives of the Wire Service Guild," including Normal Welton, the guild's administrator. This powerful union had 1,400 members in the AP and another 950 in the UPI at the time, or some 80 percent of the total newsroom staff. Welton recounted a story about how a member at UPI had at first called for a strike, but then showed pride in the machines.[59]

Bagdikian noted that there was a kind of speed paradox with the new computerized systems, with "the national news transmission network . . . still basically a voice-grade telephone or telegraph line" and set to handle mostly teletype delivered and received copy at 45 words a minute, accounting for fixes and corrections. Special high-speed lines used by about 40 of the UPI's clients and 200 of the AP's members, leased at about $180 a month per line, could receive 1,050 words a minute, and produce paper copy or computer signals at the same rate; it was also technically possible, but rare, to use equipment that could receive at 2,100 or even 3,000 or more words a minute. Please see Figure 2.1 above to see examples of the AP and UPI's systems in use.

But because most of their clients/members could not use this faster-delivered material, most were not, at that point. A few early adopters, however, had either expressed an interest or were in the process of doing so, including the Booth Newspapers, in Michigan, with about eight papers. The management there estimated they'd save about $50,000 a year along with another $120,000 from not having to pay eight compositors.[60]

However, these changes might, eventually, be more thoroughly resisted by production-plant news workers, he believed, and it was unclear how the use of a CRT/VDT that combined different workflows and processes into one operation or a couple of operations compared to the more complex and discrete work of building layouts by paste pot, or even to inputting text via Linotype, and thus to hot and then cold press operations.[61]

At this point at the *Detroit News*, for example, paper type was still used to feed a linecaster machine at the usual 14 lines a minute; but using CRT displays and OCR tech meant that deadlines could be pushed up, since a story could be written and then put on the page, in theory, within ten minutes, so that instead of an 8 a.m. deadline for an afternoon edition, copy could be sent in as late as 11 or 11:30 p.m.[62] He noted that "the outcome of these battles . . . will determine who has maximum control over the editing process and how much money owners can realize from innovations. . . . What matters is the impact on the quality of the product. Will news organizations, already fabulously profitable, shift production savings to the heart of the business – news and editorial?"[63]

As he put it, "The dream of all journalists and conscientious owners has been to free the American newspaper from being mostly a factory." While he realized, too, that the temptation from more efficient technologies, especially on the production side, would be to further cut the size of a newspaper's workforce, the goal would be to add to it, so that

> most of a paper's energy will go into covering its community and region, that leaders of news organizations will no longer be executives rewarded for their commercial and mechanical management efficiency but men and women who are essentially recorders and analysts of social and political events.[64]

One could also say that what Bagdikian was prophesying was already coming to pass, and indeed the pages of trade publications from the era suggest that many observers were already thinking ahead to what minicomput-ers (the "personal" computer had not yet been imagined, at least in terms of office or newsroom settings) could do. And yet again what he did was call for a more systematic adoption of computers not as niche devices, but as everyday production tools, for and by news workers.

Moving from OCR to VDTs

Writing nearly a decade later, and with more detachment from the American publishers who had been so keen to see Bagdikian's expectant predictions,

Anthony Smith's *Goodbye Gutenberg* shows some of the outcomes more than a decade's worth of computerization had wrought.

But Smith identified 1975 as "the year in which the bandwagon of computerization really got going," with nearly 30 companies selling computers to the newspaper industry, with what he estimated were about 1,000 minicomputers and other kinds of computers being used "in the field."[65] Even large, comparatively wealthy newspapers such as the *Detroit News*, the *Los Angeles Times* and the *Philadelphia Inquirer* made mistakes, sometimes expensive ones, with this process. And it was not just the transition of switching the locus of control from the production to the editorial side of the newspaper. A change in mindset had to occur, too.

It was one thing to adopt a mainframe (or, as increasingly was the case by the late 1960s and early 1970s, a minicomputer) to solve a few specialized problems in the production pipeline of newspaper manufacturing. It would be another matter entirely to shake up the traditional processes by which these products were built and distributed; even the most enthusiastic newspaper executives "were nervous at the time of acquiring machines that would alter the basic structure of the plant." Moving to a more purely photocomposition-based system would mean that optical scanners and computers were necessary, and not just interesting experiments.[66]

OCR, while useful for expediting the input of text, took time and training to use effectively, and could be expensive. When used badly, though, it could – ironically – slow down the flow of copy through the long chain of events from reporting to putting newspapers out on the street or on the doorsteps of suburban subscribers.

Reporters would have to learn to use "editorial 'front-end' systems . . . for normal work." Older reporters could and often did balk at the switch, which could be uncanny, from typewriters to keyboards-and-screens (still not to computers-on-desks, but through "dumb" terminals). The VDT would have to "pass from an outlandish and experimental tool to a glamorous modern necessity," and "reporters and editors had to be trained and made to feel that the instrument added to, rather than distracted from, their professionalism."[67] And that would only come from time, trial and money.

"A computer system must always be a mirror of a social structure, and in most newspaper systems the hierarchy is fairly simple," Smith noted, unless a newspaper was like the *Washington Post*, which relied less on wire copy and instead generated ample national copy of its own, and had such a large staff of hundreds of reporters and editors that the top-down nature of a smaller paper would not work as well. For this and other reasons, the *Post* was among the first to invest in smarter terminals that had some of their own local memory (a total of 250 terminals, built by Raytheon). With 300 reporters on staff, at least 200 of them could be working at any one time – the goal was to get most, if not all, of them near or on a computer. In an era when the typical access ratio of staff-to-machine was more like 2:1, this was remarkable.

But right on through the 1970s, buying and installing (and actually using) a proprietary minicomputer-and-VDT system was a customized effort, and done "with the same degree of subtlety as one might chose the furnishings of a house." It would be another decade before off-the-shelf microprocessors (i.e., what would later be called "standard systems") would be capable of competing with the Hendrix's, Harris's and Raytheon's of the early newsroom computing universe. In the meantime, the rule in the 1970s, according to Smith, was to avoid "buying systems 'off the peg' [i.e., without thinking] . . . and [to] get the whole staff into the right frame of mind for the adventure before it begins."[68]

Early digital newspaper archives

Another parallel development to OCR and then VDT for manipulating text was the storage of that text in newspaper library systems, or "morgues." These involved hybrid analog-digital formats for both storage and retrieval.[69] Smith believed that these could bring both practical research help and some monetary value to newspapers, especially old and large publications with their old files of clippings with photos only available there: "Transferred to microfiche or to on-line systems, this decaying store of knowledge can become a living asset, available to schools, universities, and other researchers."[70]

Led by the *Boston Globe*, but also the *Los Angeles Times*, the *Toronto Globe and Mail* and the *Chicago Sun-Times*, newspapers would arrange for continued efforts to put printed material on microfilm or microfiche, and then have searchable (often via accessible keyword-based) indexes, or in some cases a more fully digitized search system, prepared. With 15 million clippings dating back to the 1930s, the *Los Angeles Times*, for example, used the proprietary Zytron Data Systems Library Information System.[71] This let reporters see selected scans of microfiche sheets within about three seconds on a VDT screen, and allowed searching by first keyword and then category (i.e., op-ed, biography, interview, photo, etc.). The sheets could be printed for easier reference while a reporter worked on his or her story (note that it was still separate from the newsroom's minicomputer-VDT system). It also allowed for updates to categories of material, so that "segregation," for example, could be filed under "integration." Some limitations of the system included its cost, at $250,000 in 1980 ($787,900 in 2018 dollars), and limited memory. With the latter, it had a disk memory of 40 megabytes, which could hold the index and search program for a newspaper, but could be expanded to two gigabytes, and could hold five years of the full text of the *Los Angeles Times*'s archive if needed.

The *Boston Globe*'s archive, which held 226,000 obituaries, 800,000 photo prints, and nine million individual clippings in 700,000 physical folders, all containing material dating back to the 1880s, was on microfiche, but the paper was attempting in the late 1970s to move its current editions to a more truly digital archive via OCR, with help from the Mead Corporation's research and development team. The paper's management encouraged reporters to use the older microfiche, versus the physical folders, by putting their own work on that medium. The index-search tool employed by the *Globe* used a "keyword-in-context" method that looked at the 12 words before or after each search term. The *Globe and Mail* had a similar system, in place since the early 1970s, and built by QL Systems, based in Kingston, Ontario.[72]

The latter allowed for some statistical analysis of stories, including how many stories a particular reporter had written, and what the reporter had written about on a particular issue, arranged chronologically. The system also allowed for reporters to use one part of their VDT screen to search directly from the archive, and then another for drafting their story. It did eliminate about seven staff members from the archive, but an archival crew was needed to continue flagging data for later reference. The *Boston Globe*'s approach was similar, in that search terms were detailed and designed to be used for writing stories.[73]

The *Chicago Sun-Time*'s burgeoning digital archive provided text based on "field" searches, that included details on bylines, dates, word numbers, photos, story genres and datelines (and even corrections, as needed). Material that was typeset by its VDT-minicomputer content-management system was added to the archive on a daily basis.[74]

Having archival material available for not just outside consumers such as researchers, but for internal news staff needs, promised to save time and lead to more analytical, context-based stories (and also stories that could be written faster and with fewer errors). Before the internet, access to information for and by journalists was much more expensive. Attempts at committing newspaper archives to at least some kind of digital storage was a way to save money, in that regard.

Conclusion: from early experiments to OCR to VDTs

While the approximately 10-year period from the mid-1960s to the mid-1970s saw comparatively few mainframes and then minicomputers installed in working newsrooms, the cooperation of MIT and the ANPA, along with the growth of the latter's efforts at its Research Institute, all within the larger context of the American software and hardware industries, meant that the stage was set for newsroom computerization in a more fully realized way beginning in *c.* 1975.

Others were less convinced. Terence Day, a letter-to-the-editor writer in a November 1973 issue of *Quill*, believed that "the electronic technology" would be a

> detriment to the quality of the products of newspapers where extra time demands are permitted to infringe upon the probably already under-staffed newsrooms; and a boon to those papers where enlightened publishers recognize that they have shifted some of the burden from the back shop to the newsroom and adequately compensate with an appropriately larger news staff.[75]

The next chapter explores the computerization of the newsroom that followed at a more rapid pace through the 1980s, showing how "dumb" terminals gradually became smarter, and what impact that had on news workers' routines and thus, ultimately, their sense of control over work and sense of agency.[76] The more engagement a news worker felt with technology, that is, the more readily available, immediately applicable and therefore helpful it was to completing job tasks in a newsroom setting, the more affordances that technology provided news workers. Examining the *materiality* of newsroom technology will remain a focus of this study, as well as the path-dependent nature of that technology.

The more capable and more intrinsically embedded computer tech became (especially in the form of the microprocessor, as it replaced the minicomputer) in the form of one's "own" desktop computer (and even as that term became domesticated, and reified by ordinary news workers), the more complete newsroom computerization would become, and the more natural and normative that narrative, so that computers in newsrooms would seem almost inevitable, when, in fact, their presence (at least as observers in 2018 perceive it to be) was anything but guaranteed, and their impact far less than certain.

The drive to reduce the use of OCR and move to VDTs was partially motivated by a desire to reduce the number of steps in the news-production (and before that, editing and gathering) process. As one staff member at a small paper in California put it, "All systems involving scanners, video terminals or magnetic tape processors have one main purpose: to get rid of the second, redundant keyboarding of copy." New technology did not mean fewer workers, per se, but even if it did, the resulting leaner, more creative workforce would use "the new technology – however feared, reviled and bothersome. . . [to] have contributed to better journalism."[77] Optimistic predictions of technology use in newsrooms were the norm for the era, and the hopes pinned on VDTs were no exception.

Notes

1 Frank Van Riper, "Hot Type: In His New Book 'Recovered Memory,' Frank Van Riper Meditates on His Career in Newspapers from the 1960s to the 1980s," *Columbia Journalism Review*, Oct. 1, 2018, https://niemanreports.org/articles/hot-type/.
2 J. T. Johnson, "The Unconscious Fraud of Journalism Education: Computer Database Skills Are Essential for Serious Journalism. Why Are J-Schools Failing Us?" *Quill*, June 1992, 31. Johnson also comments, perhaps a bit grandiloquently, that "the *Tribune* had indeed recognized that a new electronic age for journalism, the beginning of the most significant period of change and opportunity since the introduction of the printed word, was upon us."
3 Kirschenbaum, *Track Changes*, 36–37.
4 Hamid R. Ekbia and Bonnie A. Nardi, *Heteromation: And Other Stories of Computing and Capitalism* (Cambridge, MA: MIT Press, 2017). Ekbia and Nardia argue that the history of computing needs to be reframed through the concept of *heteromation*, which they define as "a computer-mediated mechanism of extraction of economic value from various forms of human labor through an inclusionary logic, active engagement and invisible control," 39. While a powerful explanatory concept, I would contest the intentional implication; with some exceptions, newsroom computerization did not proceed from a planned set of goals, but was rather people-driven, reactive and, if anything, emergent. Still, understanding and appreciating stories of upheaval and loss, and reinforcing the value of human workers' struggle, is vital, and helps to motivate my own research.
5 Jim Rosenberg, "Rinehart Reflects on 40 Years of Change: Retired ANPA Vice President Stays Involved with Newspaper Technology," *Editor & Publisher*, June 16, 1990, 32, 108–109.
6 Though in the various narratives of newsroom computerization (and in the discourse of the original accounts in the trade literature), it is important to not treat the device as a mystical black box that solves problems as if by magic. Hours of programming, and with great trial and error, led to time-saving and a more organizing system. For more on the forwards-and-backwards nature of early programming efforts, see the definitive work of Martin Campbell-Kelly, especially his *From Airline Reservations to Sonic the Hedgehog: A History of the Software Industry* (Cambridge, MA: MIT Press, 2003). For the account of the *World Telegram*'s computer, see "Computer Licks Payroll Details," *Editor & Publisher*, Aug. 29, 1959, 36. The presence of computers was also seen in ads for RCA's magnetic-tape storage system, including one in the Sept. 19, 1959, issue of *Editor & Publisher*.
7 For example, the work of Louis Moyroud and René Higonnet, both French and immigrants to the United States, after WW2, led to improvements in such devices; their updates were partially adopted by some ANPA members, and first demonstrated at the 1949 ANPA convention. Their initial test machine in the United States, nicknamed "Petunia," become the Photon 200 series, developed partially along with Project Whirlwind at MIT; a further Petunia prototype, ZIP, could set 600 characters a minute but was so expensive that only the CIA and a medical library bought one. Vannevar Bush and Samuel Caldwell, at MIT, were interested in their early work, too. The transistor made some of these devices obsolete, apparently, but they were ahead of their time and again set the stage for later. See Jerome Walker, "Photocomp Inventor Tags 'Explosion' – Not Revolution," *Editor & Publisher*, June 5, 1976, 19–20.

8 Paul Martin, "Overview: Computers and Newspapers in the Mid-80's," *Editor & Publisher*, Feb. 1, 1986, 1 c, 24 c; Johnson, "The Unconscious Fraud of Journalism Education," 31–34. More on the early use of computers to wrangle stories out of big-data sets can be found in Philip Meyer's textbook series, which will be explored more later in this study. See, for example, Philip Meyer, *The New Precision Journalism* (Bloomington, IN: Indiana University Press, 1991).

9 Richard Steele, "Computers, CRT, What Next? Research Helps Newspapers," *Editor & Publisher*, June 6, 1970, 17, 78.

10 Carl F. J. Overhage and R. Joyce Harman, eds., *Intrex: The Report of a Planning Conference on Information Transfer Experiments* (Cambridge, MA: MIT Press, 1965).

11 Steele, "Computers, CRT, What Next?" 17, 78.

12 See Overhage and Harman, eds., *Intrex*, especially their committee's predictions on future incorporation of data-storage and network technology, particularly their discussion of an "on-line intellectual community," and the "Information Transfer System at MIT in 1975."

13 Steele, "Computers, CRT, What Next?" 17, 78.

14 Anonymous staff writer, "Hendrix," *Editor & Publisher*, Nov. 14, 1970, 65; Hendrix Electronics, Inc., and its first-generation VDTs benefited greatly from ANPA-MIT research, and they were built from the outside with "compatible hook-ups to wire-service lines . . . magnetic tape and disc memories, paper-tape readers and punched, hard copy printers and data sets" [*sic*] and cost $9,000 for the CRT/desk consoles alone, with a 300,000 K memory.

15 Though in some ways the term "minicomputer" was used loosely to highlight the comparatively small size of these devices versus mainframes, one key distinguisher was price. A mainframe might cost millions, between the tech support and customized programs needed to run it; it was also often used to solve specialized problems. Paul Ceruzzi points out that in contrast, minicomputers and their successors were much more accessible, helping introduce the "notion of the computer as a personal interactive device." Their small size – essentially a tall filing cabinet that contained a processor, control panel and memory; in the case of the iconic PDP-8, built by the Digital Equipment Corporation, eight cubic feet and weighing about 250 pounds – made them more feasible for adoption by newspaper factories, which already had a number of large and heavy machines to store and maintain. Note that while DEC was a dominant force in the sector of the rapidly growing (though still fairly niche) computer industry that supplied newspapers (and could offer a base-model PDP-8, with teletype terminal, for as low as $18,000), a number of competitors were emerging by the late 1960s and early 1970s. By the latter point the price of a PDP-8, as a result, would drop to closer to $10,000, or about $59,000 in 2018 dollars. See Paul Ceruzzi, *A History of Modern Computing* (Cambridge, MA: MIT Press, 2003), 125, 129–133, 191–193.

16 Anonymous staff writer, "Editors and Computers," *Editor & Publisher*, June 6, 1970, 6.

17 Steele, "Computers, CRT, What Next?" 17, 78; Richard Cichelli, "ANPA's Research Institute Played a Role in Computer Development at Newspapers," *Editor & Publisher*, Feb. 1, 1986, 16 c, 19 c; Cichelli's recollections corroborate the accounts of Steele and Rinehart. The descendent of American Newspaper Publishers Abstracting Technique (ANPAT) was Microsoft Word's "auto summary" feature, which was discontinued in the late 2000s.

18 Cichelli, "ANPA's Research Institute Played a Role," 16, 19; very roughly, about 8,000 typed characters; while seemingly small, that much memory was more than adequate for even dozens of short news briefs, which would not run more than about 500 words or so at most. See https://web.stanford.edu/class/cs101/bits-gigabytes.html for a brief explainer on bit conversion.

19 Cichelli, "ANPA's Research Institute Played a Role," 16, 19. Another early program, EasyMark, was used for photo composition.

20 U.S. Dept. of Labor, Bureau of Labor Statistics, Consumer Price Index (CPI) Inflation Calculator; from Mar. 1970 to Sept. 1978, www.bls.gov/data/inflation_calculator.htm; where possible and helpful, I will attempt to convert prices to c. 2018 for context, in this chapter and throughout this study.

21 Craig Tomkinson, "Low-Priced OCR Unit Aimed at Newspapers," *Editor & Publisher*, Mar. 21, 1970, 36; it could also be rented for $2,000 a month, or $13,200 in 2018 dollars.

22 Mostly the brainchild/work of the conference's technical director, Noel Leon; see Jim Rosenberg, "Early 'Desktop' Publishing: Demo Dispensed with Paper Tape; VTDs and OCR Deliver All-Electronic Copy to Editors," *Editor & Publisher*, Nov. 2, 1991, 16–17.

23 Anonymous staff writer, "Telcon," *Editor & Publisher*, Nov. 15, 1980, 6–7; Telcon Industries, Inc., developed its Micromark Spelling/Proofing System, which looked for mistakes with copy, including OCR-processed copy, comparing text with a 30,000-word list.

24 This was Leon; see Rosenberg, "Early 'Desktop' Publishing," 16–17.

25 Gerald B. Healey, "Despite Initial Reluctance, Newsroom Switches to OCR," *Editor & Publisher*, Oct. 13, 1973, 47, 50; in Benjamin Compaine's, *The Newspaper Industry in the 1980s: An Assessment of Economics and Technology* (White Plains, NY: Knowledge Industry Publications, Inc.), 169–170.

26 Compaine, *The Newspaper Industry in the 1980s*, 170.

27 Compaine, *The Newspaper Industry in the 1980s*, 169.

28 Craig Tomkinson, "OCR Scanning 'Live' Copy at Worcester," *Editor & Publisher*, Nov. 14, 1970, 57–58.

29 Anonymous staff writer, "Electronic System Will Produce Richmond Paper," *Editor & Publisher*, Nov. 13, 1971, 12; this was at the 144,000-circulation Richmond *Times-Dispatch* and 121,000-circulation *News Leader*.

30 William Fisher, "Cold Type Switch Improves Productivity, Staff Relations," *Editor & Publisher*, June 9, 1973, 66, 71. At the smaller (much smaller than was typical) *Benton Harbor News-Palladium* and *St. Joseph Herald-Press* in Michigan in 1973 (about 26,000 and 7,700 circulation respectively), these newspapers shared a Harris 1100 editing terminal, two 2200 video-ad layout screens and two Compuscan 170 OCR machines, with 45 IBM Selectric typewriters. Fisher, the production manager for the Palladium Publishing Company, described the above technology as "the ultimate electronic composing and editing gear." Thirty reporters had access to their own Selectrics, and the rest, it is implied, had to share. For another example of a smaller newspaper adopting OCR techniques during this era, see "Paper Speeds Production, News Flow with Automation," and "Hagadone Affiliate Features OCR in New Electronic Editorial Set-Up," *Editor & Publisher*, Aug. 11, 1973, 35, 45, which describes the use of a hybrid OCR-VDT system at the *Sioux City Journal* and Manchester, CT, *Evening Herald*, respectively.

31 Harry N. Malone, "Computer System Links 3 N.Y. Times' Newspapers," *Editor & Publisher*, Feb. 9, 1974, 34, 42.

32 Tomkinson, "OCR Scanning," 57–58.
33 Robert Crocco, "Army Times Finds Problems in Switching to OCR Input," *Editor & Publisher*, May 12, 1973, 52.
34 James J. Barrett, "Front-End Systems: Harmony or Conflict for Man-Machine Relationship?" *Editor & Publisher*, June 14, 1975, 22, 60, 62.
35 Anonymous staff writer, "Page Layout VDTs Built into Electronic System," *Editor & Publisher*, Jan. 1, 1977, 9. For more on the transition from OCR to VDT, see Dineh Moghdam, *Computers in Newspaper Publishing: User-Oriented Systems* (New York: Marcel Dekker, Inc., 1978), 85–86; because Moghdam had access to the RI's *Bulletin*, accounts from editors tasked with newsroom computerization efforts and other research material now much more difficult to acquire, her study is particularly important to understanding the transition from OCR to VDT technology.
36 Anonymous staff writer, "Planning Aids Daily in System Conversion," *Editor & Publisher*, June 11, 1977, 60, 62, 64. The 13,500-circulation paper had moved onto a proprietary Compugraphic Unified Publishing System, with eight VDT terminals and one (probably) minicomputer with four floppy disks for storage; more on such systems in the next chapter.
37 Anonymous staff writer, "A Brief History of RAND," RAND Corporation, www.rand.org/about/history/a-brief-history-of-rand.html. Bagdikian was something an ironic figure, working both in government and very much out of it, in the latter case helping secure Daniel Ellsberg's Pentagon Papers (themselves copied using a pioneering bit of technology, the Xerox copy machine) while working for the *Washington Post*.
38 Ben H. Bagdikian, *The Information Machines: Their Impact on Men and the Media* (New York: Harper & Row, 1971).
39 Warren Breed, "Social Control in the Newsroom: A Functional Analysis," *Social Forces* 33, no. 4 (1955): 326–335; also, Warren Breed, *The Newspaperman, News and Society* (Ph.D. dissertation, New York: Columbia University, 1952).
40 Bagdikian, *The Information Machines*, 104–106.
41 Bagdikian, *The Information Machines*, 191.
42 Bagdikian, *The Information Machines*, 249.
43 Bagdikian, *The Information Machines*, 212–213, 280–281, 282–283.
44 Bagdikian, *The Information Machines*, 292.
45 Bagdikian, *The Information Machines*, 92–96. In his chapter on "the newspapers & the computer," writing from the perspective of 1980, Anthony Smith, in his *Goodbye Gutenberg* (New York: Oxford University Press) writes about the *Los Angeles Times*'s collaboration with RCA on H&J computer programs using an RCA 301 as early as 1962: "Unjustified text was taken from paper tape and turned into justified text, also on paper tape, which then drove a hot-metal linecasting machine, which created neat rows of text." By 1965, the newspaper had set up a Data Processing Department and had switched to using an IBM 360/30 minicomputer; at first classified advertising but also news content was arranged this way, with unusually sized typeset still set by hand. For more on the *Los Angeles Times*'s pioneering use of computers ("the newspaper with probably the most extensive repertoire of computer-aided functions in the United States"), see pp. 97–101 of Smith.
46 Bagdikian, *The Information Machines*, 99, 101. Teletype machines had a distinctive sound and produced large sheets of paper, and so their presence was a key part of newsroom culture. They were also among the first machines to find

their role either augmented or supplemented by minicomputers. For more on that process, please see the next chapter with the growth of centralized VDT systems.

47 Bagdikian, *The Information Machines*, 111–112.
48 Bagdikian, *The Information Machines*, 113–114.
49 Ben Bagdikian, "Publishing's Quiet Revolution," *Columbia Journalism Review* (May/June 1973), 7.
50 Bagdikian, "Publishing's Quiet Revolution," 7–8. The figure of 60 percent does seem a bit optimistic, but if you counted math-heavy operations like payroll and subscriber information, it is conceivable that about half of at least larger U.S. newspapers did, in fact, use computer technology.
51 Bagdikian, "Publishing's Quiet Revolution," 8.
52 Bagdikian, "Publishing's Quiet Revolution," 8.
53 At this early stage in the use of CRT displays/VDT terminals, even the most basic actions to later readers and writers must have seemed fairly remarkable:

> "As he types, the letters appear on the screen. If he wishes to delete or add to a line he has typed, he uses a set of command keys to move a cursor – a bright oblong of light – over the place he wishes to alter, types in the change, and the screen shows these and automatically makes room for the additions or closes up for deletions. . . . If it is an urgent story he can send it to the proper desk in 'takes' by pressing a MORE key. If he writes the story as one unit he looks it over to his satisfaction, then pushes a key marked END which sends it into the computer," Bagdikian, "Publishing's Quiet Revolution," 8.

54 Bagdikian, "Publishing's Quiet Revolution," 9.
55 Bagdikian, "Publishing's Quiet Revolution," 10.
56 Bagdikian, "Publishing's Quiet Revolution," 11.
57 Bagdikian, "Publishing's Quiet Revolution," 12.
58 Bagdikian, "Publishing's Quiet Revolution," 12; Laffler was referring to his editor's "bank" or "queue," which in one particular case could contain up to 23 stories.
59 Bagdikian, "Publishing's Quiet Revolution," 13. The guild did call for the right to *not* have to retype copy from other reporters, and had some health concerns, which will be explored later, but which centered around potential injuries to wrists and eyesight.
60 Bagdikian, "Publishing's Quiet Revolution," 13.
61 Bagdikian, "Publishing's Quiet Revolution," 13.
62 Bagdikian, "Publishing's Quiet Revolution," 9. The paper still used a one-way telephone line to send copy to be set and printed – or rather planned to, at this point – at their suburban plant some 22 miles away.
63 Bagdikian, "Publishing's Quiet Revolution," 13.
64 Bagdikian, "Publishing's Quiet Revolution," 15.
65 Smith, *Goodbye Gutenberg*, 96.
66 Smith, *Goodbye Gutenberg*, 96.
67 Smith, *Goodbye Gutenberg*, 97.
68 Smith, *Goodbye Gutenberg*, 103–105.
69 Smith, *Goodbye Gutenberg*, 110–113.
70 Smith, *Goodbye Gutenberg*, 110.
71 As will be noted later, some newspapers built and even marketed their own archival-retrieval systems.
72 Smith, *Goodbye Gutenberg*, 110–113.

73 Smith, *Goodbye Gutenberg*, 110–113.
74 Smith, *Goodbye Gutenberg*, 110–113.
75 Terence L. Day, letter to the editor, "Reactions to VDTs," *Quill*, Nov. 1973, 5.
76 As the sociologist Andrew Abbott discusses in his "jurisdictional" model (within the broader sociology of work), control over work tasks is the more interesting theoretical question, versus "traits" or "benchmarks" of an occupation's professionalization project, the same being true for journalism, and in our case, I would argue, newsroom computerization.
77 Carlton R. Appleby, letter to the editor, "The New Technology," *Quill*, Nov. 1973, 6. Appleby worked at the *Daily Times-Advocate* in Escondido, Calif., and was responding to complaints about the non-humanizing nature of elements of hybrid analog-digital technology.

3 The minicomputer era

c. 1970–1982

The mid-1970s through the mid-1980s can be characterized as the approximately decade-long period when screens, and screen-based technology, truly came to newsrooms, at least at wealthier and larger newsrooms. Unlike the experiments of the late 1950s through the early 1970s, beginning in about 1975 terminals attached to minicomputers reshaped more newsrooms and their work processes faster and more thoroughly than had any other editorial technology except for the telephone and the typewriter earlier in the century.[1]

The focus in the trade literature and other then-contemporary industry accounts during this era was on "front-end systems," especially starting around 1980. In that year and the years to follow both vendors and publishers became focused on replacing, albeit slowly, traditional "paste-up" processes for layout, even as word processing dramatically impacted the work routines of most reporters and editors.[2] Other related parts of the newsgathering, editing and production process became connected, also slowly, to computerization, including the processing of early digital images, transmission of stories by satellite and the use of very early cellphones to cover the news. Some of these developments remain out of the scope of this study, but the increased adoption of VDTs in particular is emblematic of a decrease in one-off and instead reflects a rise in dedicated investment in computer technology in the 1980s.

The estimated number of VDT units in use in newsrooms jumped from only about 685 in 1973 to more than 7,000 in 1976 and more than 15,800 in 1978, while minicomputer use rose to nearly 2,000. (In many of those latter cases, one or two such minicomputers would form the center of a VDT system at a smaller newspaper, as reviewed in the last chapter.)[3] OCR scanners had in the meantime declined, reaching a peak in 1977 at about 738 (beginning with about 186 in 1973) but starting a slow decline in 1978 with 712 reported in ANPA surveys (and with a similar decline in specialized OCR typewriters, from 6,100 in 1973 to a height of 23,500 in 1977 to the start of a gradual decline in 1978 with 22,200).[4] It was hard to be both proficient at

OCR and also at VDT: most newspapers would eventually choose the latter, though OCR tech would linger into the 1980s.

A special 1973 issue on the transition from a focus on OCR to VDT, sometimes referred to as "CRT" (cathode-ray tube) technology in the Society of Professional Journalists' *Quill* explored how that process looked on the ground with rank-and-file news workers. As one observer, Robert C. Achorn, of this transition noted, with many second-generation OCR-based systems, a screen was in fact often used for editing once the scanned copy had been inputted.[5] By 1972, 155 scanners were in use, but even at early adopters such as the *Breeze Courier* in Taylorville, Illinois (with a circulation of some 8,567), their impact was mixed. "They [the OCR readers] tend to slow the editing process and the thought process in the newsroom," noted Achorn. "The material may even have to be retyped, which means another keyboarding – more time, more cost, more chance of introducing error."[6]

In contrast, VDTs

> permit a reporter or editor to 'massage' the story quite rapidly. At the push of a button, the story appears on the video screen from its computer storage. An editor, working on a keyboard at the screen, can make all the needed changes to get the story into final form. The handling of paper can be eliminated.[7]

While not a perfect replacement – an editor at the *Daytona Beach Journal* said that working on a VDT was initially 80 percent slower than using a pencil – advocates believed that the time was made up eventually in other ways.

In November 1973, United Press International (UPI) and the Associated Press were using a total of 150 "video editing terminals," already beginning to bypass the OCR process altogether, with the AP's VDTs mostly in Los Angeles and New York City. The *Detroit News* was also a pioneer with the technology.[8]

Achorn advocated for a "total system" along the lines of UPI's and AP's, and one that was composed of VDTs and OCR scanners alike (with as many as feasible of the former). But there was one side effect: "There is still . . . in every newsroom the human problem of working out the individual's relations to the machine," with one immediate effect being a literally "quiet newsroom."[9] Another impact was on the compiling and organizing of information in ways that could save dozens, if not hundreds, of hours.[10]

"The new electronic systems lend hope that a higher proportion of a newspaper's spending can go into original work, rather than duplication," Achorn argued. It was editors and rank-and-file reporters who needed to engage with computers in their newsrooms, as "the quality of the newspaper is finally determined not by the machinery but by the men and women who report and write and edit for that newspaper."[11] Training them to use technology gradually could reduce anxiety and allow for a smoother transition.

At the *Detroit News*, where 72 VDTs were in use, the associate editor tasked with tech development, Albert Abbott, noted that the typical reporter or editor was, in fact, intimidated by first using a VDT, but that "this was true of the typewriter, too. I know some old reporters who had to write out their stories in longhand first and then retype them."[12]

Echoing Achorn, another observer, citing the AP as an example of an early adopter and innovator with VDTs, said that

> in the rush to embrace the new technology, we should not lose sight of our basic purpose – to do the best possible job editorially and put out the best paper we can. We must not let the machines control us. The newspaper must believe this and the staff must know it.[13]

This theme of the need to retain control, or domesticate technology and tame it to use in newsrooms, reflects the pragmatic attitude many news workers felt about the introduction of new tools. Since they did not directly threaten their work patterns, only disrupted them (unlike mechanical workers, who felt more immediately in danger), reporters and editors tended to reskill on new devices in ways that empowered their sense of control over occupational boundaries.[14] Even early descriptions of writing on VDTs (and note that this was before more sophisticated word processing programs) highlighted the agency of the news worker:

> A newsman *writes* a story on that typewriter-like screen in front of him. Using computer command keys on the same keyboard, the writer – or the editor – can *edit* the story electronically, rather than with pencil, scissors and glue. . . . When the writer and/or editor is satisfied with the story, he can store it in the computer for later use or he can push an "execute" button on his keyboard, and wham – the story is *transmitted* directly onto the designated wire.[15] [italics in the original]

Columbia, South Carolina, was the first bureau to use a CRT display and also connect via the AP network to Atlanta, on Nov. 8, 1970. Apparently, during this process, "a staffer walked in, looked around the office and said: 'My God I'm on Star Trek'."[16]

But after a while, with practice, using it was compared to driving a car with a stick shift: "Very quickly the mechanical maneuvers become second-nature and the writer is able to give full concentration to the copy." It was unlike a Selectric or other kind of electronic typewriter; instead, "it has more the feel of a manual typewriter. Most newsmen, accosted to pounding a battered but comfortable manual typewriter, have an intense distaste for electric typewriters. One of the pleasant surprises for them is that the electronic CRT keyboard does not feel like an electric."[17]

But not everyone was enthused with either OCR or VDT technology.

Glenn Waggoner, a staff member at the Findley, Ohio, *Republican-Courier*, a 26,000-circulation daily newspaper, believed that OCR scanning in particular was a time sink, taking more time than "simple, fast rewrite and cut and paste job on copy paper."[18] Reporters just were not temperamentally suited for the work of writing, editing and layout, and needed more help, not less. Mechanical workers' jobs were being threatened in non-sustainable ways by technology, and other newsroom staff were not up to the task of replacing them:

> There seems to be no avenue of relief except adding more newsroom personnel to offset the increased editing time required. . . . There's certainly no turning back on the thousands of dollars invested in the new equipment. One editor took another newspaper job prior to our move [of locations/buildings], saying he'll return to teaching before he'll deal with scanners and the like.[19]

Still, Waggoner hoped that more reporters would advocate for technology used in ways that made sense for their jobs, not necessarily that they would resist it.[20]

Other mid- and high-level newspaper managers were less than happy with how VDTs were impacting their newsrooms. Robert Engle, the managing editor of the *Miami Herald* (and someone whose position usually had oversight of technology development), claimed that an informal in-house study at his paper showed that editing on a VDT was less efficient and potentially more error prone than working on paper, necessitating the adding of up to 20 percent more editing staff "if editing of high quality is to be maintained . . . the best editor in the world makes mistakes, and so does the best H&J computer program."[21]

In contrast, a 1978 Missouri School of Journalism study that examined 145 copy editors at 42 newspapers with VDT systems found that the differences in quality and speed were potentially negligible, or at least not statistically significant, between editing on a screen versus on paper. Half the editors surveyed said that VDT usage improved their accuracy; 61 percent said that it led to more eye fatigue (by using the screens); 60 percent said they spent *all* their editing time on the machines; 26 percent said they spent most of their time (more than 90 percent of their time); and 15 percent said they spent less than 89 percent of their time on them.[22]

A 1980 study by a researcher at the University of Arizona had more mixed results. A survey of several dozen daily newspapers in Utah, Idaho, Montana and Wyoming concluded that in "electronic newsrooms [processes slow] the editing process, even though they improve deadline flexibility and save time on production." Echoing editors of an earlier generation who called for more training in journalism programs at the college level in the use of telephones and typewriters, more time using VDTs was needed before showing up to newsrooms that used them.[23] Computerization of newspaper production at all levels was well under way, reducing "the number of steps and souls required to create the product." As one industry joke put it, someday soon a smart news worker and a computer could put out nearly the entire paper by themselves. "If that day has not arrived, and I believe it already has in the technological sense, the speed with which the concept becomes reality will be limited only by the imagination of newspaper executives and the supply of versatile people who can make it work."[24]

VDTs: from novel to (more) normal

Writing about the transition from OCR to more truly screen-based input systems and other related computer technology in the newsroom, Charles Tait, tasked with helping the managing editor of the *Baltimore Sun* with that paper's large-scale (and early) conversion to VDTs, noted that reporters went through a number of stages when faced with the prospect of using new machines:

> [1] anticipation with fear; [2] then disbelief; [3] proceeding to a high on the new technology after a short time span with the new system; [4] then disillusionment; [5] followed by partial rejection, and finally [6] the ultimate re-bounce [*sic*] to enthusiasm for the new electronic approach.[25]

Starting in 1973, and in a two-year process that culminated in one VDT for every four reporters (and one for every copy editor), some 76 VDTs arrived in the *Sun's* newsroom, centered around five Harris 2500/50 "integrated editing and composition systems." See Figure 3.1.

This made it one of the first "operational front-end [i.e., used by rank-and-file news workers] and composition system[s] on the East Coast," according to *Editor & Publisher* technology reporter Earl Wilken. "Reporters are free to use terminals located in any area of the newsroom should the VDT in their particular area be occupied," he wrote. Their terminals were mounted on swivels (rather like typewriters and telephones had first been shared during the 1920s and 1930s), with these desks bolted to the floor.

ON-LINE EDITING AND PROOFING is being done on a Harris 1100 video display terminal at Cocoa (Fla.) Today.

Figure 3.1   Craig Tomkinson, "Harris Editing CRT Features Stand-Alone, Multi-Input Design," *Editor & Publisher*, June 6, 1970, 15. While an early example, this image shows some of the advantages offered to a more VDT-oriented system, including the ability to see edits made in real time on a screen, by a reporter and from an editor.

Editors were given 11 hours of training over three days, with reporters having seven hours over two days; a 12-week period was thought of as sufficient for conversion.[26] Other newspapers tried to train technology managers, editors and reporters sufficiently before their machines arrived, in order to ease the transition. In one set of illustrative documentation used by the staff of the *Pioneer Press* in Glenview, Illinois, by the mid-1980s a technical manager for a small- to mid-sized newspaper might attend up to a full week of courses on terminal and minicomputer (and later microprocessor) operation at a manufacturer or system-assembly company like System Integrators, Inc. He or she would, in turn, be expected to conduct classes for editors and reporters back at the newspaper.[27]

Attempts to organize training and reduce news workers' anxieties concerning tech dated back to the 1970s, where it was found that dropping new devices into traditional routines could cause friction, delay and frustration.

VDT adoption throughout the 1970s

When the *Baltimore News American* purchased 20 Logicon and seven Teleram VDTs as part of a minicomputer system, William Dowd, the managing editor, noted that some of his staff "at first were dragged, kicking and screaming" into using them. But once they realized that they could send their copy to editors to be organized via "Action List," Dowd claimed that "you couldn't get them away from the machines." Control over the flow of copy seems to have been key. As Dowd put it, "I've seldom seen a person, once exposed to the VDTs, who wants to go back to a typewriter."[28]

A few years before, in 1973, at the *Augusta Chronicle and Herald* in Georgia, managing editor David Playford observed that at least 30 minutes were saved when reporters were "typing directly into a computer – and know[ing] that what you see on screen is what you get, the staffers are much more careful with their typing, thus reducing the error factor." The what-you-see-is-what-you-get factor distinguished the use of terminals from OCR readers.[29]

The exact cost of early transitions from OCR to VDT systems (or the incorporation of the latter alongside the former), however, could sometimes be unclear.

But when the *New York News* adopted a $6 million Mergenthaler Linotype Company "electronic pre-press publishing system," it received sustained attention from the newspaper trade press, with delivery slated to start in the summer of 1977 and be finished in the spring of 1978.[30] Utilizing terminals for a number of operations, not just for reporters entering their story drafts, its various programs were stored on floppy disks and a handful of hard drives, but with two dedicated databases, called Data File Processors. One of the databases would be a primary and the other a backup, and connected, in turn, to 80-megabyte storage units called Data Files, with up to five of those (two for editorial and one each for classified ads, display and production), designed for redundancy in case of power failure or hardware

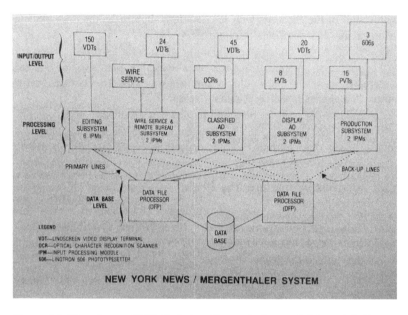

Figure 3.2 "Page Layout VDTs Built into Electronic System," *Editor & Publisher*, Jan. 1, 1977, 9.

issues. Each Linoscreen VDT would have a very limited local memory of 8 kilobytes, and essentially needed to be operated as part of the system, and not apart from it. See Figure 3.2.

Makeup, including some hyphenation and justification (again, abbreviated as "H&J") of news/editorial content, would be done on some 16 dedicated terminals. These would have the ability to display full-size versions of tabloid-sized pages, with eight stylized typefaces, with cursor controls and grids to help with setting text in place, along with a zoom feature and alternative layouts. Eight terminals would be used to make up lucrative display ads, with 20 VDTs used for inputting copy.

Eventually, devices referred to as "Graphic Tablets" would be used with the page-view terminals, to help draw the outlines on any graphic material or photos using electronic styluses; this would allow terminal operators to visualize layouts and prepare more sophisticated alternatives: "In other words, all the functions once considered strictly cut and paste will be performed electronically on the 19-inch screen of the Page View Terminal."[31]

A total of 45 VDTs would be used for all other classified ad projects, with two local "line" printers and two OCR devices; the latter's software would allow for unique character sets and also credit checks and cost quotations. Three 606 CRT phototypesetters, using digitized fonts that could set type up to 3,000 lines a minute, completed the system, with an average tabloid page, with windows left for graphics, produced at 22 seconds a page. Overall, 239 VDTs and about 14 minicomputers along with two larger computers and ten hard drives composed the system.

As noted in the previous chapter, journalism-industry analysts such as Ben Bagdikian were writing about the adoption of VDT-and-minicomputer systems early in the 1970s. The development of the UPI's "computerized information and storage and retrieval system," an investment costing the wire service over a $1 million in equipment and contracts before the installation was more or less finished by 1974, illustrates the immense cost and risk in computerization efforts prior to about 1974.[32]

One early, and expensive, VDT model was the Harris-Intertype 1100, which cost about $14,500 in June 1970, or $94,000 in 2018. It had an 8 1/2 by 11-inch display, 63-key keyboard, tape reader, tape punch and solid-state electronics and allowed an editor to work on copy inputted via paper tape, and then outputted via tape, for further processing on a teletype machine.

Developed partially with help from ANPA's Research Institute, it could display up to 8,000 characters and allowed for "scrolling" with the local, limited memory, which was described as "moving copy forward and back via keyboard command," in a one- or two-column format, approximately printed column inches, and using a 14-point, Cairo Light typeface, with serif, and adjustable brightness. For the time, it was an advanced editing tool. A cursor, a "light point appearing on the CR screen," it was explained, was "the operator's indicator of where copy modification is to take place." It was piloted at the Gannett-owned *Cocoa Today* in Florida, along with the *Ithaca Journal* in New York State. Alongside the ANPA RI input, Harris itself solicited help from news workers in the design.[33] A rival VDT device by Hendrix cost about $9,000 in November 1970, or about $58,000 today.[34]

In many cases, descriptions of VDTs centered around their similarities to TV screens, as Lenora Williamson, a technology writer for *Editor & Publisher*, demonstrated with her news briefs outlining the AP's and UPI's computerization efforts. In both cases (the AP's more decentralized approach, versus the more headquarters-centric tack taken by UPI, as outlined earlier), the wire services invested millions of dollars and years of research and development into the process of newsroom computerization.[35] But as a general rule, the cost of individual VDT units decreased through the 1970s, even as their capabilities increased. They were also increasingly "on-line," in the sense that their computing power was tied in real time to a dedicated minicomputer and disk-based storage systems. That allowed stories to be stored for more than an immediate production period, and led to early digital archiving, which will be covered more in later chapters. But the ability to manipulate not just text but also photographs and some simple graphics meant that VDTs would become much more than a kind of "super typewriter."

For example, a small daily newspaper in Kansas used five VDTs and an Extel Printer along with a Compugraphic 2961, with the VDTs costing less than $2,500 each.[36] One critical development, beyond price reduction, was the adoption of more mix-and-match VDT-minicomputer technologies by smaller newspapers, in some cases using ANPA-subsidized programs such as Layout-8 (discussed in the previous chapter).[37] In 1976, at the *Skagit Valley Herald*, a small newspaper north of Seattle, in Washington State, $185,000 bought spare parts, a 32-kilobyte hard drive (already nearly four times as large as the equivalent in *c.* 1972), a minicomputer and several VDTs, all of which doubled the speed at which pages could be set.[38] As profit margins were thinner and payroll costs even more make-or-break than on larger newspapers, investing in tech purchases was riskier for smaller publications. The fact that small-town publishers felt the technology was mature enough, and useful enough, by the mid-1970s to buy more of it is telling.

Large-scale newsroom computerizations continued into the second half of the 1970s, too, with prominent examples including the $2 million purchase (or $8.7 million in 2018) by Field Enterprises, Inc., of 17 Atex minicomputers and 100 VDTs for reporters and 50 more VDTs for editors at the *Chicago Sun-Times* and *Chicago Daily News*, starting in spring 1976.[39] The *New York Times* was similarly focused on installing second-generation VDTs. As part of its "Phase One" computerization efforts, with the installation of 48 Harris 1500-model VDTs, the eventual goal was to install 325. Of these, 31 would be in the main newsroom, eight on the foreign and national desks, four for the metro, sports and financial desks; three for the arts and leisure section; nine for the travel, book review and magazine sections; six to be used in the "telephone recording room" for transcription of called-in stories by correspondents and during broadcast events; two would be used for maintenance/development, the latter by Joyce Abbott, the "publishing systems manager." The goal was to have two VDTs for every three reporters, eventually. Among other goals: these additional screens would help break up the traditional newsroom layout and cluster relevant resources (such as the copy desk), and a raised floor would be installed to accommodate the physical cables and other infrastructure. Some of these objectives, however, would not be attained until the early 1980s.[40]

At the *Los Angeles Times*, 341 VDT terminals and 12 Tandem minicomputers, as assembled by Systems Integrators, were in place in the newsroom by the early 1980s. Some 94 more VDTs were to follow at its Orange Country, San Diego and Washington, D.C., bureaus. The focus was on making the VDT user interfaces simple, "without complicated coding," so "standard newspaper language [had] been incorporated into the series of steps needed to process a story through the editing system. . . . One copy of the writer's original story [remained] stored intact, no matter how many changes editors might make."[41]

On mid-sized newspapers, such as the 70,000-circulation *Atlantic City Press*, training was considered crucial for maximizing resources. With 24 newsroom VDTs and two more in its production department, and with two Dual Typeset-11 11/45 DEC-manufactured minicomputers with 112 kilobytes of core memory and 13 smaller 11/05 computers, with two VDTs per the latter, with 16 kilobytes of "local" memory each, reporters received 15 hours of training, and editors, 25.[42] As was common practice through the 1980s, even with "smarter" terminals and PCs, many of the screens had to be shared, with 20 VDTs in fixed positions, four in swivel, and with the latter shared by the sports/women's desks; three were dedicated to the rewrite-desk staff, two for suburban news and six for general-assignment beats.

In addition, there was one VDT each for the Sunday, editorial-page, city editor, regional editors, four on the copy desk, with one for the "slot" or head copy-editor position; the peak usage time was about 5 p.m., and the ratio of reporters to terminals was 2–1 (for the 72-person staff).[43] In 1976, the Milwaukee *Journal*, and *Sentinel*, both published by Newspapers, Inc., invested in a $1.5 million-Hendrix 3400 system, alongside a newsroom renovation. Some 62 VDTs were used at the former and 42 at the latter, with an emphasis on training for staff; ten staff members were given "[thorough] training," about 75 "intermediate" training, and 60 had a "basic" amount of instruction, with the latter course taking four hours.[44]

In Texas, seven newsrooms, from the *Fort Worth Star Telegram* and the *Dallas Times Herald* to the *Corpus Christi Caller*, were in the process of adopting VDT systems in the late 1970s, with generally positive reactions. Some staff members, however, continued to regard scanners as a stopgap tech, with one calling OCR "a time-waster and undependable."[45] A poll of 109 Texas dailies at the time showed that 31 of the 60 papers that responded used scanners and/or terminals with computerized systems, and with 29 percent saying they wanted to; one estimate claimed that 80 percent would have these systems in the next few years.[46]

In California, the San Jose *Mercury News* used VDTs built by a System/55 System Integrators, Inc. (which had built the *Los Angeles Times*'s terminals), since about 1974. The newsroom's management had opted to switch to a 65-strong Coyote VDT system. Altogether, the paper had 114 VDTs, with 36 of them being Delta Data terminals first purchased in 1973–1974 and in the process of being phased out. The goal with the interim and then eventual system was to eliminate the extra step of scanning, and to add more VDTs overall, to a total of 233, with 112 in editorial, 88 in classified ad layout/design/editing, 12 in production and even among its bureaus, with a further 14 held in reserve for spare parts and testing.[47]

VDTs in the late 1970s and early 1980s

VDT technologies continued to impact the newspaper industry into the next decade; more than OCR scanners, terminals were deeply folded into the writing and editing process. That meant further disruptions to production workers' collective bargaining power, vis-à-vis publishers, as the ITU continued to lose much of its clout. This was evident in negotiations at the *Washington Post*, in which a "landmark" 1981 contract between management and Local 101 of the Columbia Typographical Union allowed for reporters/editors to use computers to lay out pages *if* they pertained to news, but that ads or pages with ads had to be made up by unionized workers, who would get a pay raise to $643 a week.[48] The *Post* offered $25,000–$35,000 buyouts ($68,900 to about $95,400 in 2018) depending on age to union members who wanted to retire early. The deal also would phase out a "productivity leave" clause that gave union members three weeks of paid leave a year in addition to their regular four weeks due to efficiency gains with the addition of VDT and optical-scanner tech.[49]

The cost of incorporating terminals into newsroom work processes, especially if OCR technology had not been utilized, could still be substantial. The *Charleston News and Courier*, and the *Evening Post*, owned by the News & Courier Evening Post Publishing Company, in Charleston, South Carolina, spent $1.7 million in 1982 (nearly $4.5 million in 2018) on 103 VDTs, three PDP 11/70 minicomputers and two 300MB hard drives, along with 20 VDTs for their business department, to be installed in fall 1982 and providing "total editorial and classified production capabilities."[50]

While not quite microprocessors proper (covered more in the next chapter), "smarter" VDTs, including more processing power and memory, also began to appear by 1982 in some newsrooms, the first step toward less centralized and more distributed computing power.[51] For example, DEC's TMS-11 "computerized text management system" was used by the *West Chester Local News* in Pennsylvania, a 35,000-circulation daily, with ten microcomputer editing terminals and 34 VDTs.[52]

The 39,000-circulation *New Britain Herald* in Connecticut adapted a Harris 2560 copy processing system and a 2230 display advertising system, along with CRT/VDTs, in the summer of 1978. According to the managing editor, Richard Conway, most of the 23 staff members "were typing their stories directly onto the terminals."[53] Though not always universal, the more capabilities a terminal system possessed, the more quickly news workers adapted to, and appreciated, the technology. On the Lewiston, Maine, *Sun-Journal*, Ursula Albert, a reporter, said, "For me it was a love affair from the start." According to Robert Turcotte, assistant news editor, "We were so eager that we put out a complete paper with the system the first day it was installed."[54] Newspapers in the Midwest and Idaho were also enthused about the capabilities of smarter VDTs.[55]

By the end of the 1970s, there were nearly 23,000 VDTs in use by newspapers, which included most of the larger publications in the United States, with a 50 percent annual increase beginning in the late 1960s through 1981. VDTs continued to offer access to data and faster editing, but even a smaller newspaper needed "$200,000 to install a 'fully automated system' that includes twenty [VDTs] in the classified ad and editorial departments." For larger newspapers such as the *Washington Post*, that price could run as high as $8 million.[56]

Scholars and industry practitioners alike, however, predicated increased use of VDTs in the 1980s, including in broadcast newsrooms. Adoption of even basic word processing would lag behind that of print newsrooms for many years, however, into the 1980s, due to a variety of factors, including the expensive nature of existing technology.[57] Others believed that reporters and editors would use VDTs more at home, despite the expense in hardware and software required. In the words of one contemporary in 1981, "Newspaper computer systems turned hot lead typesetting into cool print, demolishing the front desk tradition with technology, all within the last decade. Home computers, enabling you to do the same thing privately, became available five years ago."[58] Some publishers were interested in parallel technologies to word processors, such as Videotex and Teletext (more interactive and more text-based data services, respectively), and their various field tests. These included Knight-Ridder's $1.5 million to $2 million, 160-household, partial color test with Bell Telephone in Coral Gables, Florida, as well as CompuServe ("a time-share computer company owned by H&R Block") and its test with 11 AP newspapers, along with QUBE, in Columbus, Ohio, with the latter costing about $11 a month after a "small installation fee."[59] While these would not ultimately take off, at least not in the same way that cable TV systems did, in the 1980s, the ability to engage more directly with subscribers had implications for news-gathering, editing and publication. If readers could get their news more customized, and more directly, eventually, through "home" VDTs, editors and reporters would both lose something of their gatekeeping role.[60]

Overall, however, the use of VDTs was mostly seen as a positive additive force in most reporters' lives (and lower-ranking, middle-management editors' lives, for that matter), allowing them to control their word processes more closely. As Mark Murphy, the city editor of the *Los Angeles Times*, put it, "I'm convinced now that working on a terminal may *add* to a reporter's creativity" [italics in the original]. "The speed of the computer has caused us to speed up other things," agreed Bob Farquhar, assistant managing editor of the Oklahoma Publishing Co., publisher of the *Daily Oklahoman* and *The Oklahoma Times*.

Farquhar went on to say that making a house ad went from taking up to three weeks to overnight, and then also two to three hours faster, once the work began; the ability to "digitize graphics," use pagination systems more effectively, and refer to "electronic libraries" would streamline both internal and external newsroom publication. The AP bureau chief in Salt Lake City, Ed Nichols, believed that page design in particular would be easier, with computerization leading to a "transfer of control within the structure of the newspaper itself."[61] More clear-eyed than their publisher-owners, these kinds of news workers would not have praised VDT-based systems if they did not believe in their potential.

Conclusion: from VDTs to microprocessors

In February 1981, the Tandy Corporation's chairperson, Phil North, gave a speech to the International Newspaper Advertising and Marketing Executive conference, predicting the need for more "electronic publishing" by newspapers to overcome $450-a-ton paper costs and rising fuel prices. "Don't be frightened to make this change. . . . I suggest that you stop thinking you are in the business of producing newspapers as defined by Webster."[62]

Among the first stories written on a word processor *and* with help from pre-internet networks was the reporting of Lawrence J. Magid, a San Francisco-based "computer columnist" for the *Los Angeles Times*. Using feedback from The Source, an early on-line community associated with *Reader's Digest* and described as a "computerized information utility," he published a story about a new IBM PC via *Real Times*, an early "electronically distributed magazine," edited in Montreal by Thomas Kashuba.[63]

Using a subgroup on The Source, "the IBM Post," an early "electronic bulletin board," and messages obtained from readers via his "electronic mailbox," Magid obtained scoops, edited and updated his story, and beat the trade press, as well as the *New York Times* and *Wall Street Journal*. Using his reader feedback, he corrected two errors, for example, in the same day using his access to the message boards.

He was also able to see about how many subscribers had read his story (within two days, some 512 people, spending an average of 5 minutes and 42 seconds reading it). That kind of analysis of readership was unheard of, for the time, and foreshadowed what was to ultimately come, with the internet. As the author of a *Columbia Journalism Review* recap of Magid's experience recounted,

> A number of new and interesting principles emerge in this preview of what electronic publishing might be like once it reaches major proportions in five or ten years, but what strikes me most is the participatory nature of what happened with this story and especially the new power exercised by its readers.

While this may strike us as naive, the ability of pre-internet (and later, early internet) networks to connect and drive engagement with readers was unprecedented:

> Through their patterns of use, readers defined the nature of the story. If the computer can continue to give voice to readers, then the technological revolution in publishing needn't be seen as a dehumanizing force. It could be just the opposite.[64]

In July 1983, the *Washington Post* experienced a major crash in its primary Raytheon VDT/minicomputer system, among the worst on record up to that point. A 15-minute delay late in the production cycle, in its second edition, prompted the impromptu use of several backup systems; the fault was eventually traced to an issue with the main disk drive, which led to a shutdown of all 12 of its primary minicomputers and an automatic shutdown of *300* VDTs, three hours before deadline, at around 7:45 p.m. With more than one reporter sharing a screen, that had a devastating impact on the ability of the paper to actually finish its print run, as 30 pages were still blank, and many of the already written stories were at least partially lost (in fact most of the news content entered via VDT since noon that day). But between hard copy saved and rewriting (from memory and notes kept by reporters), the news staff was able to re-input much of that material into its smaller, backup Harris system with about 40 VDTs, and the later print runs were salvaged. It was by the far the worst interruption in the three years the Raytheon system had been fully operational, and likely spurred management to switch to a PC-based system by the end of the 1980s.[65]

Dominique Wolton, who taught at the University of Paris, traveled the United States in the late 1970s for research for his book, *L'Information au Futur*, which included a number of observations of newsroom computerization as it was happening. As an outsider and media scholar, Wolton's thoughts on VDTs and minicomputers are helpful, if only because they serve as a check on the often-rosy (or reactive) depictions of technology in the contemporary American journalism trade press.

Wolton, writing in the first person, questioned whether or not VDTs, for example, were "just another way to attain traditional journalistic objectives, rather than something that may force a break with them." He believed, instead, that they had the potential to change the nature and organization of journalistic work.[66] Moving from a largely paper to at least a partially digitally created and delivered system would make "this creative process more abstract, involving an essentially visual, rather than a material or tactile, relationship to writing, which now occurs within the fixed space of the display screen."

Editors and reporters alike, however, insisted in his interviews with them that using VDTs would mean more control over copy. But the blurring of the lines between writing and production would, ultimately, lead to a set of changes in newsroom practices, he thought. Not having a production team, or not as large a workforce in those roles as before, meant unforeseen changes to news work were imminent, and sooner rather than later: "To what extent *should* journalists assume these technical tasks? When will their doing so begin to influence their creative work, if only because of the additional time and effort involved?" he asked.[67]

Fewer technical workers would mean that more reporters would have to engage directly with owners and managers, whereas before groups like the ITU could negotiate for significant blue-collar benefits that trickled upward, to white-collar editorial workers. Eventually, this might mean disruption to not only the kinds but also the numbers of jobs, unless workers could reskill to produce for "on-line information banks and news services designed for home video display," and "composite media systems, which will combine telecommunications, television, and the possibilities of the computer."[68]

That would also mean changes in the basic advertising-based business model supporting most newspapers at the time, as well as changing perceptions of what news and even information would be perceived to be by many consumers. "The failure to come to grips with a shift in the *idea* and *distribution* of information exposes newspapers to the risk of becoming an elite medium, leaving the electronic media to cater to the information tastes of the mass audience."[69]

In time, increasingly targeted news would become less, and not more, democratic, he believed, reinforcing social divisions. Technology tools such as VDT editing were not panaceas to these larger issues, despite the optimism pervading stories about their adoption, with the tone of many accounts of technology adoption from the era *not* focusing on how computerization would alter the organization and distribution of work and the content of news itself. American observers of newsroom technology instead noted "a tendency to confuse the two different processes at work here; to assume, that is, that the social possibilities of the new tools can be discovered by simply projecting their technical potential into social space."[70]

By the mid-1980s, terminals were a much more common sight in newsrooms, even in popular television and movie depictions. More importantly, the lived experiences of news workers were much more impacted by VDTs. As terminals allowed reporters – albeit often taking turns, due to limited access to these screens – to control their work more, they also helped to reconceptualize what it meant to create "content" for news organizations, from wire services and major daily newspapers to smaller, weekly newspapers. They would also usher in more truly "portable" reporting tools, what journalists in the twenty-first century would refer to as "mobile" journalism, in the form of VDTs that could travel, even if awkwardly, and also be connected to phone lines for data transmission. Those would quickly give way to portable PCs, that is, laptops and early devices, as well as cellphones.

These technologies, on a continuum of disruption, enhanced and added to, and did not so much upend, existing news routines. But like the telephone and car before them (and before that the telegraph and the typewriter), they changed what it meant to find, construct and publish news narratives. The stage was fully set for the arrival of more powerful, more capable microprocessors, that is, "smart" terminals. It is to their rise that the next chapter is dedicated, bringing the story of the computerization of the newsroom right up to the advent of the internet.

Notes

1 And even then, arguably newsroom computerization *was* faster than telephone adoption had been. For more on rates of adoption and impacts on news-worker affordances, see the conclusion.

2 Ernest C. Hynds, *American Newspapers in the 1980s* (New York: Hasting House Publishers, 1980), 272. It should be noted that in addition to being pro-publisher, Hynds was also very focused on the larger, more financially successful ANPA members, including members of chain newspapers, who had the resources to experiment with, and recover from, both successful and unsuccessful investments in proprietary software and hardware, in ways that smaller and/or more independent newspaper publishers were not able to keep up with, at least not until the arrival of more capable "off-the-shelf" systems and then also the internal network software, and operating systems, that allowed for the connecting and maximizing of disparately made devices beginning in the mid- to late 1980s. More of that will be covered in the next chapter. In addition to industry watchers, including the tech writers for *Editor & Publisher*, some journalism-studies scholars working in this era recognized the shifting landscape of proprietary-and-massive to off-the-shelf and nimbler, including Bruce Garrison, an associate professor at the University of Miami. See, for example, his paper on the "Computerization of the Newspaper in the 1980s," presented at the annual meeting of the Association for Education in Journalism and Mass Communication, in Corvallis, Oregon, in Aug. 1983. Garrison identified word processing, but also copy editing and then digital layout as increasingly critical to the future of newspapers, and furthermore believed that databases, the ability to represent their information in graphical form, and networks would change the nature of reporting. Already, in 1983, he could write that "reporters using microcomputers in their jobs believe the computer helps them spot information and angles other reporters do not find so easily and so quickly," 7.

3 Hynds, *American Newspapers in the 1980s*, 271. In his enthusiastic and unabashedly pro-publisher study of the newspaper industry (and actually an update to his 1975 study, *American Newspapers in the 1980s*), Hynds drew heavily on ANPA Research Institute numbers, in particular from the *R.I. Bulletin*, and specifically "Electronic Applications in ANPA-Member Newspaper Departments for 1978 (OCRs, VDTs and Computers)," from their 1979 series.

4 Hynds, *American Newspapers in the 1980s*, 270.
5 Robert C. Achorn, "Get Ready for the Newsroom Revolution," *Quill*, Nov. 1973, 14–18. As part of a special issue on early newsroom computerization efforts, Achorn's story shows their very much in-progress nature, and also the myriad paths adoption could have taken.
6 Achorn, "Get Ready for the Newsroom Revolution," 17.
7 Achorn, "Get Ready for the Newsroom Revolution," 17.
8 Supposedly, the first dedicated newspaper VDT, with a 2,400-character display, first appeared in May 1969 (Achorn, "Get Ready for the Newsroom Revolution," 17). Already, Achorn noted a trend toward smaller, 15- or 18-line VDTs, since they were "cheaper and less bulky," and allowed for more such VDTs to be connected to one newsroom system.
9 Achorn believed that while OCR still retained a great deal of utility, and could handle a high input, VDTs were good for "selective input and for editing," 18.
10 Achorn noted early experiments at the *Miami Herald*, but also in Philadelphia and New York City, with reporters using a "computer to compile facts on crime rates, school rankings and other complex subjects," 18; more on this later in the study.
11 "There is a real danger, for some of us at least, of being bemused and blinded by machinery, just because it is the first new equipment in the newsroom since the Woodstock replaced the pen. To describe the editor of the future as the supervisor of input or the principal manager of composition systems ignores his central responsibility to manage the creation of that input" (Achorn, "Get Ready for the Newsroom Revolution," 18).
12 Joseph W. Shoquist, "The People Problems," *Quill*, Nov. 1973, 23–24, 25.
13 "The People Problems," *Quill*, November 1973, 24.
14 "The VDT imposes more changes on the editorial operation than does the scanner, but that doesn't mean it has to stifle editors or reporters. A staff and management that fully understand the new technology, that have been properly training and prepared for it, will see to it that it is used to improve the newspaper, not impair it" (Shoquist, "The People Problems," 25).
15 Marty Sutphin, "Plug in to a Terminal: Faster, Neater and More Error-Free," *Quill*, Nov. 1973, 25–26. The CRT display was described as "an electronic sheet of paper on which writing and editing are done. Characters typed on the keyboard appear as white letters atop a black line. Spaces between words show as all-black segments on a line. Black letters on a white background indicate words marked for bold face," 26.
16 Sutphin, "Plug in to a Terminal," 26.
17 The AP apparently allotted just two days for training, and staff members were expected to jump right into using the tech. Sutphin, "Plug in to a Terminal," 26.
18 Glenn Waggoner, "New Technology? Give Me Back My Old Royal," *Quill*, Nov. 1973, 29–30.
19 Waggoner, "New Technology?," 30.
20 Waggoner, "New Technology?," 30.
21 Robert Engle, "Editing Found Slower on VDT," *Editor & Publisher*, Nov. 5, 1977, 28.
22 Anonymous staff writer, "Study Shows: VDT Editors Do as Well as Pencil-Paper Editors," *Editor & Publisher*, Nov. 11, 1978, 33–34.
23 Larry Kurtz, "Update on 1978 Study of VDT Newsrooms," *Editor & Publisher*, Nov. 1, 1980, 27, 29. Kurtz, an instructor at the University of Arizona, former AP bureau chief, and textbook author, completed a Ph.D. dissertation at the

University of Utah, "Videoscreen Impact on Intermountain Newspapers." He believed that "too many students still shudder at the sight of VDTs and run for the false security of the nearest typewriter, ignoring the reality that will face them when they apply for jobs."

24 Kurtz, "Update on 1978 Study of VDT Newsrooms," 29.
25 Earl W. Wilken, "Behavioral Dynamics Stressed in Front-End Conversion," *Editor & Publisher*, June 14, 1975, 22. This process and variations, some rougher and some smoother, was also noted by Compaine; see *The Newspaper Industry in the 1980s*, 169.
26 Wilken, "Behavioral Dynamics Stressed in Front-End Conversion," 23.
27 Finding Aid (2016.055) for the Paul Pierce Tandem NonStop, Living Computer Museum collection, Seattle, Washington. Note that the System/55 Coyote VDT Tandem NonStop "was put together, maintained, and trained by Systems Integrators, Inc.," and often referred to, for short, as "the Coyote VDT." Perhaps its most famous client was the *Los Angeles Times*; more on that in this and the next chapter. The museum, funded by the late Paul Allen, is one of the most underutilized resources, in this author's opinion, for media history research on computing technology. The staff allowed the author to try out a number of programs on both emulators and on original hardware that would have been native to newsrooms in the *c.* 1970s and 1980s. That experience was immeasurably helpful for understanding the "feel" of word processing programs, especially.
28 Anonymous staff writer, "Computerization Produces Newsroom Benefits," *Editor & Publisher*, Apr. 10, 1976, 48, 53. "Even one of the copy boys here has mastered it," Dowd noted (though this might speak highly of the copy boy!).
29 Tom Hils, "Georgia Newspapers Pioneer News-Orientated VDT System," *Editor & Publisher*, Nov. 10, 1973, 53, 56.
30 Anonymous staff writer, "Page Layout VDTs Built into Electronic System," *Editor & Publisher*, Jan. 1, 1977, 9. That would be nearly $25.9 million in 2018.
31 "Page Layout VDTs Built into Electronic System," 9.
32 Anonymous staff writer, "UPI Awards Contract for Automated Editing," *Editor & Publisher*, Apr. 18, 1970, 112.
33 Craig Tomkinson, "Harris Editing CRT Features Stand-Alone, Multi-Input Design," *Editor & Publisher*, June 6, 1970, 15.
34 Anonymous staff writer, "Hendrix," *Editor & Publisher*, Nov. 14, 1970, 65. This cheaper price point reflects that it was literally for the console itself, not for other peripherals, such as keyboards or input devices, which would sometimes be included in the list prices for early VDTs (though many ads did not list prices, per se, and instead encouraged interested publishers to call sales representatives for price quotes).
35 Lenora Williamson, "UPI Sets' 72 Target Date for Its Automated Service," and "AP Will Extend Regional Computer Systems in '71," *Editor & Publisher*, Feb. 20, 1971, 9. As with other tech, the wire services were keen pioneers of VDTs and computers, partially because of the sheer volume of news content they were generating at the time and had to distribute globally.
36 Anonymous staff writer, "Floppy Disc/VDT System on/Line at Kansas Paper," *Editor & Publisher*, June 14, 1975, 54.
37 Anonymous staff writer, "La. Paper Implementing New Layout-8 Program," *Editor & Publisher*, Aug. 9, 1975, 25–26. See also anonymous staff writer, "Indiana Daily Converts to 6400 System," *Editor & Publisher*, Nov. 8, 1975, 29. Another typical example was the *Bloomington Herald Telephone*, which adopted eight Hendrix VDTs in fall 1978, and the *Watertown Daily Times* in

New York State, which used 40 IBM 3270 VDTs to store, review and edit wire-service copy. See also anonymous staff writer, "VDT Systems," *Editor & Publisher*, May 7, 1977, 36; in this classified ad, a used Hendrix 5200B 8K VDT that had been purchased in September 1972 for $18,000 was being sold for $5,000; "well maintained . . . perfect to edit TTS tape or for back-up to small front-end system . . . excellent for daily or weekly with Compugraphic 2961 or 4961. . . tape perforators . . . could be used for first step into electronic publishing." The ad was placed by a Marc U. Anthony, publisher of the Scotts Bluff *Star Herald* in Nebraska.

38 Anonymous staff writer, "Newspaper Group Designs Electronic Copy System," *Editor & Publisher*, Feb. 14, 1976, 35. The anonymous author claimed that there were about 11 such small daily newspapers using similar systems around the country. It should be noted that as VDT prices slowly edged down from about $10,000–15,000 to about $2,000–3,000, purchasing such tech became much more viable for smaller news organizations and their less-robust equipment budgets. See anonymous staff writer, "Digital," *Editor & Publisher*, Mar. 20, 1976, 18–19; an ad for DEC's VT61/t VDT had a price tag of $2,950; for that you'd get a 35-pound terminal with limited local memory.

39 Anonymous staff writer, "Field to Equip Reporters and Editors with VDTs," *Editor & Publisher*, Nov. 1, 1975, 10–12. As with many such systems, reporters were to input their stories on dumb terminals, with editors retrieving the drafts from a centralized memory for editing, also on VDTs.

40 Anonymous staff writer, "N.Y. Times Embarks on News Editing System," *Editor & Publisher*, June 5, 1976, 16, 80. Women, incidentally, were at the forefront of leadership in newsrooms when it came to tech training and management, sometimes moving from copy desks and "women's sections" to supervising tech-adoption campaigns and early newspaper IT departments.

41 Anonymous staff writer, "New Editorial, Circulation Systems On-Line," *Editor & Publisher*, Aug. 7, 1982, 35. In addition, a 120,000-word dictionary was programmed into the system to provide a form of spell checking. Anthony Smith explores this installation process more thoroughly in his *Goodbye Gutenberg*.

42 Earl W. Wilken, "One-Step Changeover Goes Smoothly," *Editor & Publisher*, Nov. 8, 1975, 36–38. The average age was 33, with about 30 percent women. Clipboards were used holding copy to be typed up, next to the screens. About 50 columns, at 750 words per column, per day, were anticipated to be processed by the VDTs; "Phase Two and One Half" and then "Phase Three" would be completed starting in mid-1977, it was estimated, with more full adoption of VDTs by the early 1980s. The *Times* would eventually shift to PCs, but not until the later 1980s.

43 Wilken, "One-Step Changeover Goes Smoothly," 36–38.

44 Anonymous staff writer, "Milwaukee Papers Go Fully Electronic," *Editor & Publisher*, July 3, 1976, 69, 71, 73. See also anonymous staff writer, "Tal-Star Computer System Ordered," *Editor & Publisher*, Nov. 19, 1977, 34. The New Jersey *Register* and *Journal Courier* were also typical of mid-sized metropolitan (i.e., more urban than suburban focused) newspapers. Reporters would continue to file stories with Selectric typewriters and upload copy via scanners. The VDTs would be used by editors mostly. It would use the T-4000 and T-410 minicomputers built by Tal-Star, and would cost $1.5 million to install, or $6 million in 2018.

45 Heber Taylor, "Texas Editors Like New Technology," *Editor & Publisher*, Nov. 19, 1977, 35. One example of an editor who was not a fan of lingering

OCR-based tech was Paul LaRocque, editor of the *Bryan Eagle* in College Station, Texas.

46 Taylor, "Texas Editors Like New Technology," 35.

47 Ben Phillips, "Latest Features Built into Front End System," *Editor & Publisher*, Mar. 7, 1981, 4, 46. Eventually, three 300-MB drives would provide content storage, with two for text and a third for programs, part of a more "fault-tolerant" system that shared computing resources more efficiently. The focus on the *Mercury* system was redundancy.

48 George Brandon, "Printers' Contract Paves Way for Electronic Makeup," *Editor & Publisher*, July 4, 1981, 37. Right through the demise of the International Typographical Union in 1986, its power was substantial in American newspaper publishing. The successor union to the ITU, the Communications Workers of America, is affiliated with the American Federation of Labor and Congress of Industrial Organizations (AFL-CIO), along with the Canadian Labour Congress. "Mechanical" workers were historically paid far more than rank-and-file reporters and lower-ranking editors, at least through the heyday of the American Newspaper Guild in the 1950s through the 1980s, though a recent wave of unionization in the mid-2010s may mean that the unionization movement is regaining some of its latent strength.

49 Brandon, "Printers' Contract Paves Way for Electronic Makeup," 37.

50 Anonymous staff writer, "Harris 6000 Gets Nod from SC Dailies," *Editor & Publisher*, May 1, 1982, 58.

51 Anonymous staff writer, "Hastech Unveils First in a Family of Intelligent High-Speed VDTs," *Editor & Publisher*, June 19, 1982, 83, 92; for example the 16-bit microprocessor-powered (the Motorola 68000) "Magician" VDT system was built Hastech, Inc., based in New Hampshire.

52 Anonymous staff writer, "PA Daily Buys 34 VDT Text System," *Editor & Publisher*, Jan. 20, 1979, 2. See also anonymous staff writer, "Compare," *Editor & Publisher*, June 9, 1979, 59; in an ad for Mycro-Tek, its various systems range from one VDT at $7,795, to four for $25,380 (540,000 character memory), eight for $46,560 (20 million character memory), and 12 for $74,240, but offering some 40 million character storage (versus just 70K for one). See also anonymous staff writer, "Editor & Publisher Goes on Electronic System," *Editor & Publisher*, Sept. 20, 1980, 13; the trade publication was switching from a Mycro-Comp 1100 "editorial system" with nine VDTs attached to a Mergenthaler 202 CRT typesetter, and also incorporating the ability to transmit their final page proofs to be printed in Penn., from its various offices, including its headquarters in Chicago.

53 Anonymous staff writer, "System Puts News-Control Under Fingers of Editors," *Editor & Publisher*, June 3, 1978, 20, 64.

54 Anonymous staff writer, "Staff Rates VDT System as 'Super,'" *Editor & Publisher*, June 3, 1978, 32, 72. See also anonymous staff writer, "Microprocessor VDT System Introduced," *Editor & Publisher*, July 1, 1978, 24. Microsystems Development Corporation's VDTs were still basically screens, but with more local memory (up to 32K for up to 4,096 characters – up to about 700 words counting spaces), at $3,500 each, as well as more expensive "editor" VDTs with a microprocessor for $4,750. A state-of-the-art VDT with some local memory in a typical mid-sized newsroom could store up to about 700 words (with spaces) on a local drive or disk, but not much more.

55 Anonymous staff writer, "New Equipment," *Editor & Publisher*, Feb. 19, 1977, 34–36.

56 Jeff Sorensen and Jon Swan, "VDTs: The Overlooked Story Right in the News-room," *Columbia Journalism Review* (Jan./Feb. 1981): 32–38. Also in this par-ticular piece, in the late 1970s and early 1980s, there were concerns about the physical effects of sitting down and staring into more screens than had pre-viously been present in newsrooms, and that while the National Institute for Occupational Safety and Health (NIOSH) concluded that there wasn't an ion-izing (the bad kind that can hurt cells) radiation hazard, both the ANG and local unions/individual newspapers agreed that there were dangers to eyesight and posture, at least, from unbroken use of VDTs, especially in bad lighting (long an issue of concern to publishers/owners). About 20 papers, including the *Wash-ington Post*, *Cleveland Plain Dealer* and *Baltimore Sun*, paid for exams, while about eight papers (such as the *San Francisco Chronicle* and *Oakland Tribune*) paid for glasses for their news workers; rest breaks were being used at the *Min-neapolis Tribune* and *Star*, *St. Paul Pioneer Press* and the Lynn, Massachusetts, *Item* (note these papers were more on the progressive end when it came to how they treated their news workers at the time).

57 Phillip O. Keirstead, "Broadcasting Adopts the Computer," *Quill*, Apr. 1981, 10–13. Keirstead describes the general lack of specifically computer tech by broadcast newsrooms (behind that of print newsrooms), despite the more tech-dependent nature of broadcasting, noting two major exceptions, in the form of Radio Free Europe/Radio Liberty, based in Munich, then West Germany, and KCBS NewsRadio in San Francisco. He mentions a few other examples of early adopters, including the use of a TRS-80 Level II $2,500 Radio Shack computer by Howard Kelly, a news director at WTLV in Jacksonville, Florida, to "assist his staff with information processing." Ideally, however, a computer would help reporters and producers alike better organize and track information, including superimposed words on the screen. The head of the news dept. at KCBS NewsRadio in San Francisco said, "I've got some people who've been here literally since '42 and '43. They would go to the typewriter (when the system crashed [parens in the original]) . . . they'd be typing away and they'd keep an eye on the screen, and when the cursor came back, they swung back, which means they had been weaned off typewriters." In another telling com-ment, however, Spencer Kinard, news director of the KSL stations in Salt Lake City, said, "The one thing about computers that really bothers me . . . is that even though you may lay out a couple of hundred thousand dollars in capital investment to buy the hardware and to pay for the software, you still must pay a monthly updating fee because they're the only ones that have the source code for that software." Michelle Bille, from WQAD, said: "The computer people are computer experts, they're not news experts, and that's where their problems come in; they did not understand our needs as news people." Still, for a few thousand dollars, one powerful desktop computer could do more for a broad-cast newsroom than even a far more expensive, $100K–$500K system; quality, the author noted, might be the driving force that led to more TV/radio stations adopting computer tech, along with some money savings (though spending money to make money was necessary, it was noted): "If this interest has a broad enough base, then computerized newsrooms will become common. If the desire for quality is limited, then the next few years will bring us only a few, quite expensive installations." Much more can and should be written about broadcast newsrooms and their computerization during the Cold War, but that is beyond the scope of this study.

58 P. Gregory Springer, "Farewell, My Lovely (Typewriter)," *Quill*, Apr. 1981, 14–15. Springer said that dedicated word processing systems could come with service fees/charges of up to $1,000 a year, with electronic typewriters that could store up to a page in their very limited memories costing between $2,000 and $10,000. He recommended hiring a consultant, and then hunting down the various computer components, or peripherals, such as a printer and keyboard, but also a 64K memory board, disk drives, power supply, and motherboard (he himself tracked down a "Sol" built by a young enthusiast). He mentions a number of possible word processing programs, including Electronic Pencil, WordStar, Apple Writer, Scripsit, Magic Wand and Auto Scribe, with different benefits and drawbacks (though these are not as spelled out), and as also mentioned in *Track Changes*. Springer settled on WordStar because of its relative sophistication (ability to handle rewriting, but also complicated tasks like constructing a newsletter); his older printer cost $500 and could print 15 characters per second (even then slow, as some systems could print up to 300 but cost about $3,000).

59 Cecilia Fielding and William C. Porter, "Time to Turn on the Newspaper," *Quill*, Apr. 1981, 16–18. As reviewed briefly in the introduction and conclusion, various data services did not turn significant profits prior to the civilian internet and web browsers, partially due to the expense, including fees associated with hardware and subscriptions, but also due to the limited utility of devices in the home, at least as contrasted to more conventional mediums.

60 Fielding and Porter, "Time to Turn on the Newspaper," 17–18.

61 Fielding and Porter, "Time to Turn on the Newspaper," 17–18. In Nichols's words: "The newsroom now has total control of the news product." Nancy Kyle, the layout editor at the *Miami Herald*, said that it would no longer be possible to blame mistakes "on the backshop."

62 Bill Goede, "Tandy Chief Advises Move to Electronic News," *Editor & Publisher*, Feb. 7, 1981, 13. Tandy owned Radio Shack at the time, and produced the influential TRS-80 "Tandy" PC that was among the first such machines adopted for use in newsrooms, including a more "portable" version that could transmit data via a modem, and which is covered elsewhere in this study.

63 Ralph Whitehead, Jr., "Slouching Toward Sunnyvale: Interactive Journalism Racks Up the First Computer Scoop," *Columbia Journalism Review*, Oct. 1983, 27–28. Whitehead was a journalism instructor at the University of Massachusetts Amherst. The subject of his story, Magid, went on to a successful career as a technology journalist, writing textbooks and producing commentary on the burgeoning role Silicon Valley had on the rest of the planet.

64 Whitehead, Jr., "Slouching Toward Sunnyvale," 27–28.

65 Anonymous staff writer, "Main Computer Fails at Washington Post," *Editor & Publisher*, July 16, 1983, 16.

66 Dominique Wolton, "Do You Love Your VDT?" *Columbia Journalism Review* (July/Aug. 1979): 36–39. Wolton's summary of his research was translated by Victoria Ortiz; as Wolton put it, "The fact that the transition from paper to computers is bound to modify the process of intellectual creation was never mentioned," 37. Wolton contrasted his experiences in the United States with trips to four European countries' newsrooms.

67 Wolton, "Do You Love Your VDT?" 37.

68 Wolton, "Do You Love Your VDT?" 37.

69 Wolton, "Do You Love Your VDT?" 38.

70 Wolton, "Do You Love Your VDT?" 39.

4 The microprocessor era
c. 1982–1992

After about 1985, more powerful desktop computers gave reporters and editors access to not only content-management systems, word processing and, in some cases, early digital archives, but also to powerful research tools, including databases, that meant their journalism could be more searching, thorough and contextual. Portable computing tech was also coming more fully into its own. Reporters had access to terminals while on the road in ways that are not too dissimilar to the present. Perhaps the biggest shift with newsroom technology, however, was that by the end of the decade and the start of the 1990s, in the immediate run-up to the launch of the civilian internet and its (eventual) adoption by newspapers, access to "smart" terminals was normalized (though not ubiquitous), even as such access continued to cause disruption of work routines and definitions of journalistic work were already beginning to change in profound ways. Some of these changes were not easy. "New technology can cause reluctance, fears or anxieties among staff members," noted one researcher in 1986. "It was only a short time ago, for example, that VDTs – now taken for granted by most staffers – were viewed with some trepidation."[1]

Perhaps a better way to think of the arrival of the internet, then, is not so much as one single disruption of the newspaper industry, and newsrooms, but as part of a series of disruptions, some more profound than others, some more containable within narratives of labor and news work, and some dead-ending before they were to have changed everything (witness the launch and failure of various Videotex and Teletext efforts, contrasted to the experiences of other Western countries, including France and its Minitel, or Britain and its Post Office-centric efforts).[2]

From "dumb" to "smart" terminals

In September 1987, reporters at the Rochester *Democrat and Chronicle* in New York State had a problem. Their colleagues were stealing open

VDTs whenever they turned their back. Michelle Williams spoofed this bad behavior in a satirical advice column that contained some real counsel, too.[3]

Writing in the guise of an advice-seeker, "Seeing Red in Rochester" set the scene:

> The other day I was on deadline, and I desperately needed a VDT. Of course, every other reporter in the newsroom was on deadline and desperately needed a VDT, too.
>
> So began the daily scramble for a VDT, which sometimes can be so rare.
>
> On this particular day once the dust settled, guess who was without a VDT. But no sooner had I finished cursing technology – we never had to go through this during the plentiful days of typewriters – when I spotted an unclaimed VDT in the corner of the newsroom. Since the notes needed for my story were on the other side of the newsroom on my desk, I staked my claim by signing on and typing in a byline for good measure. I then ran to my desk to grab my notes and, don't you know, in the split second that it took me to fly across the room and back, my VDT was gone?
>
> Gone, I tell you.[4]

The reporter asks about how best to deal with the situation next time, besides "bringing my cousins from Chicago to take care of this thieving reporter," and Williams then responds. She agrees that "in the days when Royals and Underwoods reigned, there was none of this circling and swooping for computers like buzzards gone off a diet," and generally every reporter had their own typewriter (at least by the middle of the century). The lingering cost of VDTs and then desktop computers made sharing them a necessity for many publishers. That meant that "in newspapers all across the United States of America, fellow reporters are coming into the newsroom all ready to write after a hard day of finding The Truth, only to find themselves facing the more difficult job of finding a tube."[5]

What Williams proposes is a series of technology-etiquette guidelines, or what she referred to as "tube etiquette," so that between their meetings with bosses, workshops, reporting outings and errands, they could share their limited access to screens. For the first point, she notes that reporters should not think of having "'my' tube," since "if God meant for each reporter to have a VDT, he would have never put VDTs on tables that swivel," even if each reporter typically could expect to have a desk of their own.

When it came to leaving the newsroom for the day, it was one thing to camp out with notes and clippings, especially on one side of a shared desk, but if a reporter arrived and needed a terminal that you were not using, you should give it up, or if you needed a screen and they needed more desk space, "a chair and your lap make excellent desk substitutes." Williams also explained, more seriously, that "it is generally understood that editors and police reporters have unlimited access to nearby tubes – the latter due to the nature of the beat and the need to have a VDT, phone, radios and scanners all within an arm's reach," but that other reporters were not entitled to screens. Such individuals were "tube hog[s]" and could be properly shunned.

If you were not on deadline, you should give up your VDT, or if you were working on the same story, take turns. If you had to turn a fellow reporter away and have them search for an available screen "in the hinterlands of the newsroom," the least you could do was answer their phone for them (this being before pagers). It was also reasonable to be kicked off your VDT if you left your machine for about "15 minutes on deadline and 30 minutes all other times," though these times were fairly arbitrary. Leaving for longer, or leaving the building, meant that you were "within your rights to sign off anyone . . . It doesn't matter if the reporter left to plug the parking meter with quarters, grab lunch, or visit a sick grandmother." In order to not rile one's peers too much, however, Williams warned that "this use-it-or-lose-it strategy is applicable only on deadline."

It was considered very bad form to sign someone off if they were just using the bathroom, getting coffee or visiting the newspaper archive: "then you'd be slime to sign off the reporter and take over the tube" under those circumstances. In time, and with practice, one could develop a "VDT-seeking radar" to tease out which computer was truly free and which one was not; though when in doubt, Williams always advised asking: "You're a reporter, remember?"[6]

The slow shift to desktop computers in newsrooms in the late 1980s and early 1990s

In the introduction to a special issue on personal computers published by *Editor & Publisher* in September 1988, technology reporter George Garneau defined the move away from "groups of proprietary 'dumb' terminals – cathode-ray tubes and keyboards with no processing or memory of their own – plugged into shared central processing units containing memory and software," to "PC systems: standardized off-the-shelf workstations that can run standard software standing alone or, linked in networks, can perform in editorial and advertising production systems – handling text, graphics and pagination – or in business and data processing systems," as the new "fourth wave" in newsroom computerization, and as part of a $40-billion-a-year industry. To put it another way, the future was in smart terminals.[7]

Citing other industry observers, Garneau believed that "the trend is driven by newspapers pressing to take advantage of the burgeoning processing power of microcomputers [i.e., microprocessors] and to put it directly in the hands of newsroom personnel, classified ad takers and scores of workers and executives in every newspaper department."

Cheaper and faster computers had begun to emerge on the market in a big way beginning in about 1985–1986, and forced vendors to offer more "open" systems, compatible with formerly rivals' hardware and software: "Big-system vendors have to rewrite complex software for PCs while maintaining existing proprietary systems. Vendors have to prove they can provide the functionality, speed and volume required for big newspapers."[8]

PCs were also thought of as more flexible, efficient and possibly easier to use than big centralized systems; but up through about 1988, "no PC system [had] proven itself at a large, metropolitan paper."[9] They were also referred to as "standard platforms," and Macs as well as IBM machines, and their imitators were referred to as "PCs" in the trade literature, and used increasingly for layout purposes, along with word processing and research.[10]

And while "generations" of computers had already come and gone from newsrooms by the late 1980s, it was generally agreed that PCs and microprocessors were part of a "third wave," with the first having been mainframes, and the second minicomputers. As these third-wave machines became more commonplace, so did their operating systems and networking software, including DOS, OS/2 and UNIX, respectively, linking formerly disparate systems.[11]

Software remained a major expense for PC-based systems, with reference programs costing $600 for a single-user version and up to $5,000 for multiple users; a small, six-terminal system, with 640 megabytes of data storage and an extensive, 2.3 gigabyte backup hard drive, could cost up to about $35,000 in 1988.[12]

Throughout the decade, newspaper manufacturing conferences highlighted the increasing importance of PCs in daily operations. The initial goal was to supplement minicomputer systems, but within a few years industry observers predicted that microprocessors, even the comparatively boutique Apple Macintosh (such as Apple IIe's) could complete many of the functions once only handled by mainframes. Dropping price points also helped with this belief.[13]

Some larger newspapers like the St. Louis *Globe-Democrat* were still installing large VDT-minicomputer systems as late as 1984.[14] But gradually falling prices and increased capability meant that smaller newspapers, including the 80 percent of the approximately 1,700 daily newspapers at the time that were less than 50,000 in circulation, found smart terminals an economical way to move to a screen-based workflow.[15]

"PCs do text editing as well or better than many of the larger systems on the market and also open a window to *any* [emphasis in the original] computing that needs to be done," observed Stephen Waters, the vice president of the *Rome Daily Sentinel* in New York State, a paper with a 20,000-daily circulation. Waters saw continuity between VDTs and PCs, but also a chance for a kind of positive disruption, a more economical, flexible option. "Our newspaper needs all the functions of the big-city newspapers. . . . Our PC-based system has all the function at less than 60 percent of the cost," he observed. Newsroom computers were moving from being able to do one or two tasks well to a multifunction tool.[16]

In Tennessee, the publisher of the *Cookeville Herald-Citizen* agreed; Joseph Albrecht, working with a $20,000 budget, was able to purchase software, a Radio Shack Model II to run it, and a DMP printer, all for $19,000. "We call them 'personal computers,' but don't let the stigma of the name lead you to believe they are single-user systems or limited in function."[17]

That stigma had to do with the belief that smaller microprocessors, and software written for hobbyists and even other kinds of businesses, just could not stand up to the daily rigors, and volume, of the content-flow and management required by daily newspapers. Over time, however, that prejudice would fade.[18]

Part of that acceptance came as a result of the conference circuit, including the recurring ANPA technology summits in June. Once called "Mechanical Conferences," and dating back to the 1920s and 1930s, they brought together vendors and publishers to showcase the latest in computer software and hardware, along with more traditional technology such as printing and distribution tools. In coverage of these events, and recaps, owners and editors would often call for more savvy deployment of computer tech, especially with news-editing processes.[19]

Publishers were ultimately swayed by early adopters, however, and their successor stories, including the *Kansas City Star*'s three-month trial run of an Apple Macintosh-based system to make up ads, graphics and marketing material. Despite initial reluctance to use "home computers" that had only proven themselves previously in "newsletter production," skeptics gradually came to see that PCs at least could supplement tried-and-true VDT terminals.[20]

New challenges with PC-based newsroom systems

Due to their use of off-the-shelf, sometimes fairly ersatz peripherals and unsecure networks, newspapers found themselves vulnerable to early PC-based viruses, especially those introduced via disks or other portable media. In May 1988, one of the first major examples of such a virus impacted the

Providence Journal-Bulletin, which had a reputation for cutting-edge use of outside databases in its reporting. An infected outside disk brought by a reporter by accident, and carrying the so-called Pakistani "brain virus," corrupted a number of the paper's internal files. Half of the terminals at the paper were IBM or IBM-clone machines, with the rest being made by Atex (which was supposedly less prone to viruses), but the damage was done. But the fix was fairly simple: the tech-support staff overwrote the boot instructions for the content-management system and cleaned up the infected disks before further harm could be done.

The newsroom was then warned to "practice safe computer with Write-Protect Discs," and to carry them in purses and wallets, via signs in the newsroom. *Editor & Publisher* noted that "the potential for destruction has become particularly acute as more newspapers turn to personal computers for their editorial computer systems," and that even NATO and Apple computers had begun to be infected by various computer viruses. The newspaper industry had been relatively immune, but that would begin to change, and special issues dedicated to PC systems would often include tips on how to secure against the threat of infection.[21] How to recover from the inevitable infection rapidly became a subgenre in the trade literature, too.[22]

Operating systems, scalability and the infrastructure of reporters having their "own" computers

The *New York Times* moved away from its previously more proprietary systems starting in 1988, following the example set by the *Houston Chronicle* with that newsroom's use of CText and UNIX, and the *Chicago Tribune* with its OS/2, opting to go with Atex to install a comprehensive system using IBM machines and UNIX. According to the *Time*'s spokesperson Bill Adler, quoted in an *Editor & Publisher* story at the time, the paper had already begun moving toward more-capable desktop computers.

"We have some PCs . . . in some of the partial systems already here," Adler said. "It's a matter of being comfortable with that technology and feeling it's got the flexibility for something like this where you are going to possibly need to go in different directions than you think you might at the beginning."

To that end, the *Times* was planning on using PC Writer software and its IBM Model 50s and then also 70s and 80s. The typical reporter's PC would still have fairly minimal memory, but even that was a step up from having to be connected to a central minicomputer. It should be noted that apart from the *Washington Post*, the *Los Angeles Times* and the *Chicago Tribune*, along with the wire services, the *Times* had perhaps the single most ambitious goal for PC adoption in the late 1980s, with up to 1,400 individual workstations anticipated.[23]

Another large-scale adoption of PCs was at the *Chicago Tribune*, which purchased 400 CText, Inc., IBM workstations. The resulting surge in electricity and air-conditioning demands required a retooling of the fourth-floor newsroom in the Tribune Tower, according to the "systems editor," Paul Dix.[24] Each of its IBM PCs was to run on OS/2 and possess an independent, 40-megabyte drive (larger in storage but smaller in physical size than some smaller newspaper's entire "drum" style hard drives a decade before), replacing its older Hendrix system for $4.2 million ($8.9 million in 2018), not counting additional hardware expenses.[25] Such systems required expensive software purchases, too. The *New York Times* spent $200 per machine on its Atex, IBM PS/2 and AIX operating-system-running machines; that, along with the hardware mentioned above, ran the project, ultimately, to about $22 million.[26]

But news organizations large and small believed the second major tech overhaul in a generation was worth it, if only for the greater flexibility brought by "fourth-wave" systems. While "earlier generations of electronic typesetting systems" allowed reporters and editors to manipulate text on screens, IT directors such as Richard Martin on newspapers such as the *Washington Post* thought that PCs could "imbue reporters with powers over information that ink-stained wretches of bygone years never imagined when they pounded typewriters and cradled telephone handsets against their shoulder[s]." This was a tool that was "not just a word processor."[27]

These devices would empower bureaus to become more connected to main newsrooms.[28] "Standard systems" were less and less tied to one major supplier, and could interface with hardware and software made by IBM and Macintosh alike.[29] Savvy suppliers, including these latter two companies, focused on interoperability.[30]

PCs were so powerful, in fact, that reporters and editors, used to larger and louder minicomputers, were sometimes prone to unplugging them when they needed to leave them on. Emblematic of their less-intimidating nature, as they were smaller and quieter, it was hard to take them seriously, though in some cases they were more powerful than mainframes built less than 30 years prior.[31] Some columnists began bringing their PCs to work from home, a phenomenon that will be explored more in the next chapter, and that caused some friction with editors. Some newspapers began offering computer-skills classes as a perk.[32] In time, a publisher could presume that his or her workers were using computers at home, and could bring that experience to the newsroom.

"Digital darkrooms": early digital photography

VDT technology was also impacting the handling of photography. Echoing the earlier partnership between MIT and the ANPA, a proof-of-concept

"Electronic Darkroom" (later contrasted to the UPI's rival "digital darkroom") system was developed for the Associated Press with help from a team at MIT in the late 1970s. Using a PDP-11/40, with hardware to be installed at the AP's headquarters in NYC, including a second 64K PDP-11/35, it had a "20 million computer words of memory" disk that could store 30 photos at a time and display them "flicker free."[33] While crude even by the standards of the late 1980s, the cost-savings potential spurred more research in an era when sending faxed pages could cost a news organization hundreds of dollars.[34]

The AP's research and development manager, Blant Kimbell, argued for the centrality in the new workspace for "the picture in digital form, subject to computer program control and video display for editorial judgment." As Dave Bown, a spokesperson and vice president for the AP, put it,

> We want to introduce this technology carefully. The departure from the old ways is more dramatic in this case than when VDTs were introduced into newsrooms. The parallel between what a newsman accomplished on a typewriter and what he did on the screen was exact: in both cases he simply wrote a story. The system neither added to or subtracted from the quality of his work.

The goal was to expand the digital wirephoto system to the AP's regional hubs, so about six to eight such centers would have a similar layout, with the AP wanting to connect them via "high-speed digital links" and with "two minutes or less per picture" being the transmission speed. This distributed network would contrast with later efforts by the AP's long-term rival, United Press International.[35]

Reuters followed suit with its News Pictures Terminal, which used an NCR PC-8 microprocessor and could interface with AP and UPI transmission standards. The *New York Times*, *New York Post* and *Newsday* were early adopters.[36] A more advanced AP system, the "Leaf," involved portable sender/receiver units that weight 21 pounds and were designed to take advantage of improvements in capacity and speed.[37] The AP planned to supply nearly 1,000 U.S. dailies with this technology, and sought to take advantage of a steady, if slow, use of digital photography by major newspapers. The system was designed to be used by a variety of other news organizations, including Agence France-Presse (AFP), and work with a variety of hardware.[38] The AP had a number of competitors, of course, besides UPI and Reuters, with these early systems, including Agence France-Presse (AFP), System Integrators, Inc., Sony and Kodak. The AP had the advantage of a deep bench of clients, along with pioneering photo-databases.

Early experiments with portable-transmission tech included the Scitex Corporation's 110-point, $100,000, digital-photo color scanner, used by

USA Today and *U.S. News & World Report* for their coverage of the 1984 Summer Olympics.[39] But even about seven years later, the *Sacramento Bee* was optimistically attempting to shift to handling most of its photos digitally, and thereby save material costs by up to 25 percent.[40] The trend, most industry watchers predicted, was an eventual move (not really accomplished until the late 2000s) to digital photography.[41] There were lingering concerns about format durability.[42] And only a small number of images could be stored by even more advanced systems, through 1992.[43] Alongside these pragmatic concerns, there were worries by some experts about the ability to fake photos.[44] Still, better storage and faster transmission speeds seemed promising, as did storage of photos.[45]

From "portable" to "mobile" reporting technology

"Portable" VDTs had been used to cover major sporting events, elections, conventions or other one-off news-generating occurrences since the 1970s. Teleram was a major manufacturer of such devices, with its P-1800 Portable Terminal designed to work with OCR readers.[46] Newspapers used these devices to extend their news coverage, and some, like the Indiana, Pennsylvania, *Gazette*, which deployed 11 Teleram's Portables, considered them superior to phoning in copy or using portable fax machines.[47] Some of the challenges with these systems included the fact that "calling" the newsroom on portable terminals often tied up a phone line, and data transmission could be as slow as 150 baud (or as high as 9600); the *Gazette* Telerams were used to report on NCAA basketball finals, but also more mundane stories like the Indiana Assembly.

In the early 1980s, variations on the popular TRS-80 Radio Shack "Model 100 Portable Workstation" cost $659.95 for an 8-kilobyte local memory, $819.95 for a 24K, and $929.95 for a 32K (or $1,600, $2,000, or $2,300, respectively, in 2018).[48] Despite their high cost, they allowed reporters to cover court cases and other events that had previously required writing only *after* an event, and not *during*. The ability to do the latter should not be underestimated. The four-pound, "book-sized" Model 100 could be used to takes notes and then transmit rough drafts of a story without having to "call in" as much detail (back at the newsroom, the story would be edited on a VDT; see Figure 4.1).[49]

Tony Zona, the city editor of the *Erie Daily Times*, in Erie, Pennsylvania, noted that

> we pick up a lot more direct quotes with the portables. . . . And it saves a great deal of time. Now the reporter doesn't have to write notes in longhand and then type them into a story or dictate the story over the phone. His original keystroke is captured and utilized.

ERIE DAILY TIMES city editor, Tony Zona, demonstrates the Radio Shack Model 100, with DEC's VT-61 in the background.

Figure 4.1   Jack Grazier, "New Portable Computers Change the Daily Grind of Beat Reporting," *Editor & Publisher*, July 2, 1983, 26.

Stories could be filed later, could include more details, and did not tie up as many staff members. Vicki Sanfilippo, a courthouse reporter, agreed, with just a 20-minute learning curve. Sanfilippo would sometimes take her portable home at night in case she was called in for breaking news.[50]

Some portable VDTs utilized what was referred to as "bubble memory," or cassette-tape-like cartridges.[51] Supplementing these portables were more advanced radio phones.[52] These, in turn, would be supplemented by first pagers, and then early cellphones. The latter were still primarily car-based in the 1980s, but that would change by the mid-1990s.[53]

But the appearance of more truly "mobile" computing devices in the later 1970s and early 1980s meant that reporters could take their computers with them. An example was the Osborne 1, which weighed 25 pounds, cost about $1,795 ($4,600 in 2018), and could transmit text with a $200 modem, or $100 with a "smart terminal." The default program was WordStar, and stories could also be stored on a disk for later. Rival devices by Sony, Epson and KayPro were similarly pricey. Less pricey "but difficult to use as text terminals" were the Radio Shack PC-1, the Sharp 1211, and the Radio Shack PC-2/Sharp 1500, which cost up to about $1,140 each, and the Panasonic/Quasar "Link," which used a phone cradle to hook into a modem for sending text.[54] Even on the cheaper end, a Radio Shack Tandy 102 "portable computer" that came in at three pounds and primarily did just some basic word processing cost $499 (or $1,100 in 2018).[55]

Word processing efforts at home may have also led to newsroom innovations, as reporters brought work to their home offices and then also on the road. Even using a TRS-80 or Apple II or III, and their various off-the-shelf peripheral options, however, could be prohibitively expensive. A reporter wanting to write more at home could expect to spend up to $2,500 ($6,400 in 2018) on hardware and software.[56] Many reporters preferred to leave their work at the office unless their newspaper could subsidize their investments in such devices.

While smaller newspapers thought of portable VDTs as ways to save money and report more efficiently, larger newspapers were also keen on their use. In 1982, for example, under the leadership of Elise Ross, the *Times*'s vice president for information systems, some 60 "portable" terminals were used by correspondents.[57] The market for small portables had greatly expanded by this point, with relatively unknown manufacturers getting in on the action.[58] Papers like the *San Diego Tribune* were already experienced at using these devices to cover breaking news.[59] The advantage to using portable devices was in both the reach of reporters sending back news, but also in the speed and accuracy of such accounts. The *Los Angeles Times*, itself no stranger to innovation, used P-1800 Telerams to cover local elections starting in 1976; sending in updates took as little as 15 minutes, beating fax technology and even the ability to phone stories in.[60]

Trade-press articles about laptops, in contrast, emphasized their ability to go from home to newsroom and then on the road.[61] A "conventional workhorse" could weigh "under 10 lbs" and a "high-end product" could weigh 12–20 lbs, and range up to $10,000 (similar to a high-end desktop system, which could cost between about $10,000 and $15,000 in 1988, or $21,000–$31,000 in 2018). But for research, longer stories or the use of graphics, laptops were considered unbeatable, and no longer just "luggable."[62]

Staff members at *USA Today* had started using laptops as early as July 1984, in coverage of the Democratic National Convention in Atlanta. In the latter case, a Toshiba 3100 running PC News Layout, with input from reporters using "on-site Atex equipment," was used to help put out daily updates. The 3100 was a 15 lb "portable." One tech writer predicted that it "won't be long before true portables, if not laptops, accompany graphics reporters or artists the way TRS-80 models have long traveled with reporters and the Toshiba went on assignments."[63]

By the end of 1989, however, improvements, including decreasing weight, more local memory, better displays and, critically, better batteries meant that laptops were an increasingly viable option for reporting outside the newsroom. Despite these advancements, however, desktop computers would remain superior through the 1990s.[64]

Conclusion: normalizing the "smart" terminal in newsrooms

For the typical news worker, who may or may not have had access to a computer at home (and most did not, unless they were wealthy, pursued freelancing or were computer hobbyists in their spare time), having a smarter desktop computer changed the relationship they had with their bosses, their peers and their sources.[65] The PC's affordances were such that reporters and editors alike could do more and faster than had their immediate predecessors, even those working with VDTs. An actual computer at one's disposal, even one processing a modest amount of local memory and processing power (say, a few megabytes of hard-drive space and 16-kilobyte processor), could still do more than whole teams of researchers could do a generation before, between access to databases, programs and early digital records from a newspaper's own "morgue."

If it did not entirely disrupt the newsroom work hierarchy, it certainly changed it, flattening power dynamics between bosses and workers, connecting reporters more to their sources and readers, and leading to a different kind of journalism, one more like ours than, for example, the journalism of the early Cold War, reliant as that had been on official sources and institutional knowledge to fill in the gaps in the record of events.

It is hard to convey the difference a desktop made, and would continue to make, for the ordinary rank-and-file reporters (and low-level editors) of the latter 1980s. Perhaps the difference in capability between a flip phone and a smartphone might be a helpful analogy. Both allowed a reporter in the 2000s to do their work remotely, but the latter meant that work could be better on an order of magnitude.[66] Knowing that one had as much access to the newsroom's resources physically in that space, as well as out, through portable reporting technology, was a powerful extension of journalistic identity. The internet would accelerate this process.

Notes

1 Fredric F. Endres, "Daily Newspaper Utilization of Computer Data Bases," *Newspaper Research Journal* 7, no. 2 (Winter 1986): 29–35. In his study, Endres discusses the use of "computer-accessed data bases," through a survey of his own, and a survey of other surveys. This line is from p. 33. More on the use of databases and early networks can be found in the next chapter.
2 For more on these parallel paths (and those not taken in the U.S. and Canada, in contrast) in the 1980s, see Julien Mailland and Kevin Mailland, *Minitel: Welcome to the Internet* (Cambridge, MA: MIT Press, 2017), and Anthony Smith, *Goodbye Gutenberg* (New York: Oxford University Press, 1980), which has a fairly significant section on the British Post Office's extended experiments with Prestel, an interactive news and information service.
3 Michelle Williams, "Shop Talk at Thirty: Newsroom Etiquette and VDTs," *Editor & Publisher*, Sept. 26, 1987, 48, 64.
4 Williams, "Shop Talk at Thirty," 64.
5 Williams, "Shop Talk at Thirty," 64.
6 Williams, "Shop Talk at Thirty," 64.
7 George Garneau, "Personal Computers – the Fourth Wave," *Editor & Publisher*, Sept. 3, 1988, 1, 4.
8 Garneau, "Personal Computers – the Fourth Wave," 4.
9 Garneau, "Personal Computers – the Fourth Wave," 4.
10 Mark Fitzgerald, "Newspapers Systems to PCs: You're Invited! Once Frozen Out by Proprietary Pre-Press Systems Vendors, Personal Computers Are Now Welcomed into Every Major Newspaper Computer System," *Editor & Publisher*, Sept. 3, 1988, 14–15.
11 Anonymous staff writer, "Macs Go Mainstream: SII Is Acquiring Rights to the Entire Line of DTI's Macintosh-Based Publishing Products for Exclusive Marketing to Larger U.S. Newspapers," *Editor & Publisher*, June 10, 1989, 14, 15, 144. The author of this trade-publication piece believed that the Macintosh II, IIx and IIXc, for example, were a part of this latest wave, and represented how Macs were moving from being a "standalone artist's box" and more of a true "intelligent terminal." Note that there was increasing discussion of integrating different proprietary systems through operating systems and network software during this era, despite the initial reluctance of manufactures to make that happen – more on this phenomenon elsewhere.
12 Anonymous staff writer, "On the Supply Side . . .", *Editor & Publisher*, June 11, 1988, 90, 94. A 1280x960 resolution, advanced VDT built by Viking could cost $2,395, or $7,395 with MS-DOS-based word processing software installed; this is contrasted with a $15,995 Compugraphic desktop publishing system (though price points like the latter, to be fair, sometimes included multiple PCs in a bundle). Ads for basic word processing and accounting software, also common in newsrooms during the late 1980s, show price points ranging widely, from $50 to $500 per license, depending on the brand and sophistication, and often ordered via catalogs.
13 George Garneau, "PCs Grab the Spotlight," *Editor & Publisher*, Mar. 22, 1986, 28. For example, the Apple-based Concept Publishing Systems of Beaver Dam, Wisconsin, was offering its two-terminal option for $16,000 and its five-terminal version for $43,000; the Intrepid, an IBM-compatible system with MS-DOS, sold in 18-, 32-, and 48-terminal system options at prices ranging from $60,000 to $250,000.

14 Anonymous staff writer, "Weekend Accomplishment," *Editor & Publisher*, June 9, 1984, 52, 70; in this case a Compugraphic 64-VDT system over a two-day period, to minimize disruption of regular workflow. A fairly typical centralized system, it had a 300MB hard drive and two larger processors.

15 George Garneau, "The PC Revolution: Personal Computers and PC-Driven Laser Typesetters Are Quietly Revolutionizing Small Newspapers by Offering a Cheaper Alternative," *Editor & Publisher*, July 27, 1985, 30–32.

16 Garneau, "The PC Revolution," 30–31.

17 Garneau, "The PC Revolution," 32.

18 See, for example, Anonymous staff writer, "Washington Daily 'Computerizes' by Adding Three PCs," *Editor & Publisher*, Jan. 11, 1986, 29. The author of this set of news briefs strikes an odd kind of teasing tone, but also highlights how the *Anchorage Daily News* and *Ketchikan Daily News* were making use of so-called "fat Macs" (likely customized versions of Macintosh desktops with larger 512K RAM storage) in their newsrooms. Even such a very small newspaper as the 3,000-circulation *Sunnyside Daily News* in Washington State had purchased three Apple MacIntosh computers and an Apple Laserwriter in Yakima for its regular staff of two.

19 M.L. Stein, "Newspaper Exec Offers Technological Advice," *Editor & Publisher*, June 21, 1986, 36, 120. Typical was the admonition of Kenneth Bronson, vice president of Affiliated Communications, Stauffer Communications, in Topeka, Kansas, who warned that the newspaper industry "hasn't even started to grasp" the impact of computerization: "The clock is running and we had better get to work," 120.

20 Anonymous staff writer, "Kansas City Star Begins In-Depth Test of PCs," *Editor & Publisher*, June 21, 1986, 46. It also helped that word processing programs, formerly fairly boutique and designed for the casual user, or dedicated novelist, were becoming robust enough, and cheap enough, to work well for the average news worker, including WordPerfect and then the ubiquitous Microsoft Word, launched in 1983 and already through several iterations of development by the mid-1980s. Eventually the latter would achieve market dominance on the order of 90 percent. See Martin Campbell-Kelly, *From Airline Reservations to Sonic the Hedgehog: A History of the Software Industry* (Cambridge, MA: MIT Press, 2003), 254–56. It should be noted, however, that news workers had been using basic text-editing software (often proprietary to a manufacturer such as Hendrix or Harris) on their VDTs since the early 1970s. In time word processing software would run in parallel to content-management systems on newspapers, sometimes a part of it, sometimes installed separately, but increasingly a routinized part of one's day as an editor and reporter by the end of the 1980s and start of the 1990s. For much more on this topic as it pertained to fiction writers during the era, see Matthew Kirschenbaum, *Track Changes: A Literary History of Word Processing* (Cambridge, MA: Harvard University Press, 2016).

21 Mark Fitzgerald, "Computer 'Virus' Hits First U.S. Newspaper," *Editor & Publisher*, May 21, 1988, 22. See also Mark Fitzgerald, "Avoiding Virus Infection," *Editor & Publisher*, Sept. 3, 1988, 41, and Jim Rosenberg, "'Virus Attacks': Are Newspaper PC Systems Susceptible?" *Editor & Publisher*, Sept. 3, 1988, 19, 40; both these latter pieces appeared in the annual September special issue (not to be confused with the June issue that covered the industry more broadly). A number of early articles on this issue quote a young security-minded programmer named John McAfee.

22 Jim Rosenberg, "Coping with a PC Virus: How the Memphis Commercial Appeal Handled a Computer Infection," *Editor & Publisher*, Sept. 2, 1989, 8, 10.

23 Jim Rosenberg, "New York Times Going to PCs," *Editor & Publisher*, Aug. 6, 1988, 30, 32. It should also be noted that while the *Times* was a national trend-setter in news content and practices, it was not necessarily in newsroom technology. Smaller newspapers routinely adopted the kinds of tech that the Gray Lady would also later adopt, once they seemed to have proven themselves. See also "Personal Computers," from the Sept. 3, 1988, issue of *Editor & Publisher*.

24 George Garneau, "The Pros and Cons of PC Systems: Smaller Newspapers Are Converting to Personal Computer Systems in Large Numbers, but Many of the Bigger Papers Are Hitting Some Snags," *Editor & Publisher*, July 15, 1989, 26. One worry in the large-scale push to move into PC-centric systems was shared by Sharon Bibb, *USA Today*'s assistant systems editor, who believed that "we must protect newspaper people from becoming news mechanics."

25 Anonymous staff writer, "Chicago Tribune to Convert to PC-Based Editorial System," *Editor & Publisher*, June 18, 1988, 13.

26 Garneau, "The Pros and Cons of PC Systems," 26.

27 George Garneau, "PC Systems Become Workbenches for Newspapers," *Editor & Publisher*, Sept. 2, 1989, 16, 27. About 200 of the paper's approximately 500 reporters had PCs at home, and freelancers were increasingly turning in copy typed up on PCs, replacing their older SII (installed *c.* 1984–1985) and Raytheon (*c.* 1980) "hulking" systems.

28 Mark Fitzgerald, "PCs and News Bureaus: Bureaus Are Getting That Downtown Newsroom Feel," *Editor & Publisher*, Sept. 2, 1989, 17, 26.

29 Jim Rosenberg, Mark Fitzgerald and George Garneau, "Integrating Standard Platforms: Variety Proliferates in Editorial and Advertising Front-End Systems, Ad Makeup Terminals and Electronic Darkrooms," *Editor & Publisher*, June 16, 1990, 13, 14–15, 50–51, 55–56, 58–59.

30 Jim Rosenberg, "Unlikely Alliance: PCs, Macs Still Compete, but IBM, Apple Join Forces for Future Development," *Editor & Publisher*, July 20, 1991, 15, 39. Rosenberg believed that PC desktops such as those built by Sun, IBM, DEC and HP were more truly "workstation" computers, vs. the Apple line at the time; note that he calls the former "reduced instruction set computing," or RISC, machines.

31 Jim Rosenberg, "Personal or Professional? Microcomputers Evolve into Powerful Publishing Platforms," *Editor & Publisher*, Nov. 3, 1990, 1, 28.

32 Jim Rosenberg, "Newsday Holds PC Classes: Staffers Learn What They Need to Work at Home on PCs," *Editor & Publisher*, Nov. 3, 1990, 6.

33 The MIT team was led by Dr. William F. Schrieber, along with Donald Troxel, the "father of the electronic darkroom," with Schrieber known for his work on Laserphoto. Work had been done on the system since about 1970, as digital photography was considered a long-term, not necessarily a short-term, outcome of research projects and even proof-of-concepts efforts like the first-generation MIT-AP project. "AP's New Digital Darkroom Breaks Ground," *Editor & Publisher*, June 11, 1977, 15, 64. See also "Equipment News Section: Digital Darkroom Will Deliver UPI Customers Better Quality Pictures," *Editor & Publisher*, June 6, 1981, 14, 36. Under development since Sept. 1979, it cost UPI and its corporate partner, Amecon LIF Divison (formerly Datalog) of Litton Industries, some $1.25 million, and was to be sold for $250,000 to $300,000. It could store up to 202 8 x 10-inch pictures, on two 300MB drives with 101 photos

each; seven photos could be sent and received at the same time; also captions could be written, edited and sent with the photos. A total of 16 Intel 8612A 16-bit processors were used, one for graphics, one for "queue control," and one each for the seven incoming/outgoing photos. An 8 x 10-inch photo could be scanned in three to four minutes, at 240 rpm. The monitors had more options for controlling cropping, shading and enlargement than typical screens did for the era; pictures could be rotated, too.

34 Anonymous staff writer, "Equipment News Section: Digital Facsimile Units Process Copy at Canadian Economic Meeting," *Editor & Publisher*, Aug. 15, 1981, 24, 26. Journalists from the UK, Japan, France, West Germany and the Netherlands used fax-sent copy in their coverage of an economic summit in Ottawa, Canada. Even with faxing, the savings was marked between newer digital versus traditional fax, with the use of a Rapicom 1500, at $3 a minute, for example from Canada to Japan, with 83 pages of copy costing $249 (vs. something more like $747 on a slower device); it also allowed for hand-drawn characters, helpful with the *kanji* used in Japan.

35 The system had an analog control console and video screen (and minicomputer) but would be house away from the traditional wirephoto operations desk. "AP's New Digital Darkroom Breaks Ground," 15. See also David E. Herbert, "Equipment News Section: Digitalizing and Storing Graphics in the AP Electronic Darkroom," *Editor & Publisher*, Mar. 6, 1982, 26, 28–29.

36 George Garneau, "PC-Based Electronic Darkroom," *Editor & Publisher*, Apr. 4, 1987, 60, 77.

37 Robert J. Salgado, "Color Negative News Photos," *Editor & Publisher*, Feb. 24, 1990, 12–13, 44–45. Rival devices included Nikon's NT 20000U 35-mm Direct Telephoto Transmitter, and the T/One's Phoenix digital photo transmitter.

38 Jim Rosenberg, Mark Fitzgerald and George Garneau, "Integrating Standard Platforms," 13, 14–15, 50–51, 55–56, 58–59. Essentially, as long as a fairly universally compatible operating or network-software system, such as UNIX, was present, the AP – and to a lesser extent UPI, with its less-successful system – wanted photo-transmission tech to be generally as agnostic as possible in terms of compatibility. Though digital photography is a bit beyond the scope of this study, it was a parallel technology, along with cellphones, that helped to lead to more truly mobile journalism. See also George Garneau, "UPI Scraps Pyxys," *Editor & Publisher*, June 11, 1988, 13, 152; despite two trial runs at the *Memphis Commercial Appeal* and the *Houston Post*, it had not advanced past that stage due to ownership turmoil at the wire service in the late 1980s. Also, it should be noted that in addition to the AFP, Deutsche Presse-Agentur was experimenting with digital photography. See "The Digital Photograph: Deutsche Presse-Agentur Installs First Electronic Picture Desk," *Editor & Publisher*, Nov. 19, 1983, 242–245, 27.

39 Anonymous staff writer, "Transportable Color Scanner Introduced," *Editor & Publisher*, June 16, 1984, 10, 32. Transmission costs ranged from $1,000 to $4,000 per month, and then also $1,000 an hour based on half-hour increments. Lower-resolution photos would be sent first, and then requested higher-res versions would be sent, to save money.

40 Anonymous staff writer, "Sacramento Bee Handles Most Photos Digitally," *Editor & Publisher*, Apr. 27, 1991, 28. The paper used hardware/software by Crosfield Newsline in its picture desk, along with two Macintosh IIfx computers, a Kodak XL7700 color printer, Linotronic L530, and with the Mac's having

32 megabytes of RAM, and 600MB hard drives, along with a "SuperMac" and two other monitors, with 24 bits for color. There was an additional hard drive with 45MB cartridges, and a Sharp JX600 flatbed scanner and Nikeon LS3500 film scanner.

41 Jim Rosenberg, "Electronic Picture Processing," *Editor & Publisher*, May 4, 1991, 82, 84–85.

42 Jim Rosenberg, "Enduring Data – Disappearing Pictures: What Happens to Pictures in a Digital World Where Information Lasts Longer Than Systems Needed to Retrieve It?" *Editor & Publisher*, May 4, 1991, 86.

43 Anonymous staff writer, "Nikon Electronic Imaging," *Editor & Publisher*, June 6, 1992. An ad for the Nikon NT-3000 digital photo transmitter showcased its ability to run a "self-contained workstation," with a keyboard and mouse for captions and basic editor, along with the ability to print contact sheets of low-resolution images for editors and the ability to store up to 80 compressed images. Weighing 17.6 lbs, "it slides easily under an airline seat or into an overhead compartment."

44 Tony Kelly, "Manipulating Reality: Digital Alteration of Photos Discussed at Poynter Seminar," *Editor & Publisher*, June 8, 1991, 16–17.

45 George Garneau, "Picture Desk Update: Digital Deliver, Electronic Darkrooms Soon to Be Standard for News Photos," *Editor & Publisher*, Feb. 24, 1990, 1, 4–5, 46. The estimated cost of installing the AP's PhotoStream system at 50 bureaus and with about 950 members ran up to $30 million; a cheaper system would cost at $30,000 a piece, per newspaper. See also George Garneau, "Getting Photos Faster: AP Readies Its New Digital Satellite Delivery System That Will Cut the Time It Takes to Transmit a Picture from 10 Minutes Now to One Minute," *Editor & Publisher*, June 6, 1987, 72, 126–127. Garneau clarifies that the MIT-ANPA collaboration had been going on since about 1977. Only parts of the AP's network were truly digital at this point, the author noted, and "digital darkroom" tech was considered still pretty pricey, at $40,000 to $200,000 to get started; digital storage was seen as a big challenge, though storage on CDs was expected to make that less onerous. Parallel camera technology, such as that being experimented with by Sony and Cannon, along with scanner tech, was considered key, too.

46 Anonymous staff writer, "Portable VDT Linked to OCR Converter," *Editor & Publisher*, June 14, 1975, 23.

47 Anonymous staff writer, "Remote News Sent by Portable VDT," *Editor & Publisher*, June 5, 1976, 44. Working with a Hendrix 6500 system in the main newsroom, Teleram would remain a major player in portable reporting tech through the 1980s. See also anonymous staff writer, "Teleram," *Editor & Publisher*, June 11, 1983, 37. Its Teleram 3100 "portable computer" would weigh in at 8.75 pounds, with 5–10 hour battery life, built-in teleText software and 128K or 256K "bubble" memory, and it was designed to be "an adjunct to our present computer system."

48 Anonymous staff writer, "The Computer Express," *Editor & Publisher*, June 18, 1983, 47.

49 Jack Grazier, "New Portable Computers Change the Daily Grind of Beat Reporting," *Editor & Publisher*, July 2, 1983, 26–27, 29. The *Erie Daily Times*, in Erie, Penn., was among the smaller newspapers that experimented with the use of these devices; Grazier was an editor at the paper.

50 Grazier, "New Portable Computers Change the Daily Grind of Beat Reporting," 26. A 10-column-inch story took less than five minutes to file, versus 10–15

minutes via the rewrite process; "No more tying up two reporters for one story, since the computer eliminates the need for a typist back at the office," 27. The paper's publisher, Michael Mead, predicted, "You'll take your machine where your work is, and no one will really know when you're working except by your output. It's really going to change the way we look at things. People might well ask to be paid in terms of quality and quantity of output, instead of on a time-basis," 29.

51 Anonymous staff writer, "Xitron," *Editor & Publisher*, June 6, 1981, 53. Dorian Bowen at the Living Computer Museum in Seattle, Washington, speculated that this was "non-volatile," i.e., local and removable, memory. This particular terminal had 32K "bubble" cassettes, a 12K display and a built-in acoustic coupler for telephone connections for transmitting stories. "It is light weight [*sic*] and briefcase size (fits easily under an airplane seat)." See also anonymous staff writer, "Portable Text-Editing VDT Powered by External Rechargeable Battery," *Editor & Publisher*, Dec. 19, 1981, 23; the Newsman 1, a "portable text-editing VDT terminal," weighed 16 pounds, came with a then-standard acoustic coupler/modem along with a 24,000-character memory that could retain "data when the terminal power source is removed through the use of an internal lithium battery," had a 7-inch diagonal screen and also had a word processing program pre-installed.

52 Anonymous staff writer, "Portable Phone Is Wireless," *Editor & Publisher*, July 3, 1976, 89. An experimental, short-range (10-mile) "wireless portable telephone" weighing 45 ounces and basically a small radio-telephone was thought to have potential for use by reporters, sending via phone lines "data to computers."

53 "Motorola," *Columbia Journalism Review* (May/June 1983): 3–4; noted ad for early DYNA T*A*C portable car phone, "cellular mobile/portable phone system," weighing "a mere 28 ounces"; tested in Baltimore and Washington at that time.

54 Glenn A. Hart, "Journalism and the New Electronics: Portable Computers and Terminals," *Columbia Journalism Review* (Mar./Apr. 1983): 1–3, 4–7. In this special ad section sponsored by the Electronic Industries Association/Consumer Electronics Group, the Sony Typecorder and the VSC Corporation's $199 tape recorder are featured. Note that the Typecorder could also store and edit text, and cost $1,000; a rival device from Epson, the HX-20, cost $800. Phone cradles, or adopters, allowed reporters to use telephones to send text, albeit slowly (300- to 500-word news stories would take at least about five minutes to transmit, under even ideal conditions).

55 Anonymous staff writer, "The Tandy 102: Try One on for Size," *Editor & Publisher*, Jan. 10, 1987, 2; like many such devices by the end of the decade, it could transmit text via its built-in modem back to a newsroom.

56 Ivan Berger, "Journalism and the New Electronics: Typing onto Television: The Wonders of Word Processing," *Columbia Journalism Review* (Mar./Apr. 1983): 1–3, 4–7. Berger, an editor at *Audio Magazine*, described word processors for reporters as a tool that was "the current rage among freelancers," or "mysterious," or "expensive," or "like sportscars," but potentially "saving labor . . . With a word processor, your words aren't printed on a little screen. They merely float there. You can change them, add to them, correct their spelling, move blocks of them around. . . . On a word processor, you simply keep typing. If a word grows too long to fit onto the end of the line, it 'wraps around' to start a new line. If you make an error, backspace and type over it. If you leave something out, go back and put it in. If you delete something, the other words flow back into the hole

you've left." Berger talks about how word processing programs let you find and replace, create form letters and check spelling, as well as customize fonts, add boldface or italicize. He also mentions Perfect Writer, WordStar and Select as examples of programs. As Berger put it, "Just as there is no 'perfect' typewriter for all people, there is no perfect word processing system. If you wait for one, the cost of programs and computers will come down. And they'll acquire some of the extra features you might want. But you will have denied yourself the benefits of word processing in the meantime."

57 Andrew Radolf, "Women Lead Information Revolution," *Editor & Publisher*, Jan. 16, 1982, 17. Ross had been on the job since 1979, but before that, since 1977, had been director of systems planning. She started at the *Times* as project manager of the paper's internal database, its Information Bank, in 1973. Ross indicated that the *Times* spent "tens of millions of dollars" on computer systems by the early 1980s. The paper was exceptionally wired, even for the time, with 400 Harris Corp.-built news terminals.

58 See, for example, anonymous staff writer, "Scrib Gets the News in Print While It's Still News," *Editor & Publisher*, June 2, 1979, 51. The "Scrib" was an 18-pound CRT editing terminal with a keyboard, tape deck, batteries and a telephone coupler, and built by Bobst Graphics, Inc., part of Varisystems. It was part of a growing – if still really niche – part of the market for VDT/CRT units that could, in theory at least, be used outside the newsroom to report. See also anonymous staff writer, "Telecom's Ambassador Portable Terminal," *Editor & Publisher*, Apr. 5, 1980, 30; and anonymous staff writer, "Teleram," *Editor & Publisher*, Apr. 5, 1980. In both cases, the focus was on extending news coverage via technology, in ways that were reminiscent of telephones and cars in the 1930s and 1940s.

59 Anonymous staff writer, "Editorial System Speeds Coverage of Air Disaster," *Editor & Publisher*, Oct. 13, 1979, 58–60. Remotely filed stories could be edited in the main newsroom, editors could look at stories that had been submitted, and layout software helped with story placement and in particular with story length. Reporters had access to 32 TI Silent 765 portable printing terminals with "non-volatile bubble memory and a telephone modem." The paper still used some scanning tech before final uploading for editing on the then 198,000 daily circulation paper, 58.

60 Wilson Lock, "Portable Sending Computer Eases Reporting Deadlines," *Editor & Publisher*, June 18, 1977, 37, 40. Lock believed that, despite its limitations (mainly its weight and some fragility when transporting), it was "the forerunner of things to come," especially if the devices got smaller and lighter.

61 Jim Rosenberg, "Laptops Much Improved: Faster, Brighter with Much More Memory and Many More Features," *Editor & Publisher*, Sept. 3, 1988, 8–9.

62 Rosenberg, "Laptops Much Improved," 8–9.

63 Rosenberg, "Laptops Much Improved," 8–9; using an Intel 80286 processor with 720KB and a 20MB hard drive on disks, it was part of the paper's "Jetcapade" team. So expensive, however, were the Toshibas that they were often seatbelted for convenience and safety.

64 Jim Rosenberg, "Growing Market for Laptops: Many More Models of Powerful Portables; Color Around the Corner," *Editor & Publisher*, Sept. 2, 1989, 6, 34. A Zenith 5.9 lb MinisPort cost between $1,600 and $2,800, a Toshiba $1,400; note that "notebook" was also being used to describe them even at this fairly early point; "small portable scanner/transmitters" were also in development, to help photographers send their images in faster.

65 And by "typical" I really do mean the kind of reporter or middle-management editor who would have worked at a mid-sized metropolitan newspaper, and who would have made a modest middle-class income that would not have allowed for the extravagance, usually, of a $2,000–$3,000 purchase of a home PC system (even if those prices would drop to a more reasonable $500–$1,500 range by the early 1990s). My own father, a test pilot and a fan of computing (having owned and tinkered with a Commodore 64), thought he had made a sensible purchase of a Pentium 133 PC in *c*. 1992 for about $1,200. My mother was not as convinced of the bargain.

66 As will be discussed further in the next chapter and the conclusion, however, and as media historian Benjamin Peters has cautioned, "new" capacities are profoundly hard to contextualize. See Benjamin Peters, "And Lead Us Not into Thinking the New Is New: A Bibliographic Case for New Media History," *New Media & Society* 11, no. 1–2 (2009).

5 Rise of the internet and the "full" computerization of the newsroom

By the early 1990s, and right before the internet age began to impact newspapers in the form of early sites, message boards and electronic emails, newsroom computerization was a reality, as ratios of desktops to reporters continued to decrease, the use of databases, layout software and even digital photography was increasingly included in everyday work routines and computers became as regular a part of the newsrooms as teletypes and typewriters had been a generation before. In some ways, the disruptive effects of computing had reached a kind of apex, a short lull, before the ultimate disruption to business models and reporting alike arrived with the internet by the late 1990s and early 2000s.

As the nature of newsrooms shifted ever more firmly away from their production-based heritage and toward a future in which computerized tools were changing what it meant to be a news worker, some editors were worried about a lack of investment in hiring and training.

To that end, in the fall of 1992, Edward Miller, the former editor and publisher of the *Morning Call* in Allentown, Pennsylvania, called for a more flexible, audience-driven management structure for newsrooms in response to technology adoption, especially as the traditional, hierarchical methods of more factory-style organization became increasingly outdated.[1]

Before, newspapers had been "organized as a collection of tribes, especially within the newsroom." Indeed, Miller noted, "Henry Ford would be proud of us. . . . Equally debilitating is the 25-year-old trend of moving the work of what had been 'production' into the newsrooms, with no offsetting increase in editorial manpower." The lack of new people with the time and ability to do layout, typesetting, graphic design and digital photography was becoming a liability.

> By all logic, newsroom staffing should have grown in the 1980s to accommodate this increased burden. It didn't, and economic conditions make catchup [*sic*] growth unlikely any time soon. . . . Stress is an epidemic, with no relief in sight.[2]

Miller proposed that design (via what he called "the attitude of the planner") would help newsroom staff members think creatively about job roles and making the most of new technology tools in the 1990s.[3] In time, more clearly *new* roles would emerge, including dedicated layout/design editors whose job it would be to use software for their work.[4] However, at least one observer believed that despite advances in "desktop publishing," it would take until the mid-1990s for PCs to be used extensively for layout.[5]

In the meantime, a major shift had occurred in how newspapers bought their computing resources. No longer did System Integrators and other suppliers remain supreme; much smaller vendors, such as Gateway, or older companies with established loyalties, such as Tandy, fought for market share.

A major obstacle to System Integrators' attempt to continue to compete in the later "fourth wave in publishing systems" with its latest-generation Coyote VDTs (along with older legacy systems by Atex, Raytheon and others) was price. What had once been state of the art in the early to mid-1980s had become less attractive compared to off-the-shelf, less-intensely proprietary PCs/Macs. At $20,000 per station/worker to purchase and install/set up, proprietary system vendors just had a harder case to make compared to a more ersatz PC, which might cost $1,000–$2,000 per similar station (though arguably with far less capability).[6]

If a typical mid-sized metropolitan newspaper needed at least 50–100 such systems, a cheaper order of magnitude was hard to compete with, and as corporate ownership of newsrooms became more common, bottom-line considerations became more, not less, important.[7] Computerization was a major infrastructure challenge for newsrooms even before the internet, but the start-up costs for using computers went from massive (millions) to manageable (thousands) at even the smallest weekly newspaper. But beyond their increasing presence, the newfound utility of PCs as research tools was a final disruptive effect of newsroom computerization.

The PC and its disruptive impact in the early 1990s: a new, if limited, reporting tool

Precisely because PCs were computers in their own right, and not reliant on a centralized minicomputer system for their processing power (and to a lesser extent, memory), they were the perfect tools for those enterprising reporters and editors who wanted to use them to do deeper journalism via databases, analysis of government records and pre-internet networks that included message boards and forums.

The latter included CompuServe, whose "electronic message service" allowed photographers to troubleshoot technical issues, share jobs and offer tips.[8] CompuServe's message boards, along with The Well, another popular "computer bulletin board" used system operators (or "sysops") as forum moderators. These boards and others could be used as places to cultivate sources, get quotes or story ideas by reporters. Costing up to $5 to $15, using these boards required planning and access to America Online, Prodigy or Genie, all early message-board hosts.[9] Of course, reader feedback and engagement would become increasingly common as the internet became a fully civilian and commercially accessible service via the World Wide Web, but that is worthy of its own story.[10]

More immediately, on pioneering newspapers such as the Providence *Journal-Bulletin*, the *Boston Globe*, the *Detroit Free Press*, the *Philadelphia*

Figure 5.1   Doug Borgstedt, "The Fourth Estate," *Editor & Publisher*, Sept. 13, 1986, 4. A number of cartoons from the era show anxieties associated with, and surrounding, technology adoption in newsrooms.

Inquirer, and others, reporters-turned-journalism-educators such as Elliot Jaspin were using personal computers to analyze mainframe-sized databases."[11] Jaspin left the *Journal-Bulletin* to help start the Missouri Institute for Computer-Assisted Reporting at the Missouri School of Journalism, one of the first such centers on using computers to analyze large data sets. Dropping PC prices helped to normalize their use as research tools – for $6,000, or $10,800 in 2018, one could buy enough computing power to outsize many mainframe computers of the 1950s and 1960s, with an additional storage unit that cost $3,000 ($5,400 in 2018) and $800 in software ($1,400 in 2018).[12] For a fraction of the cost of larger computers (less than about a tenth of a $100,000–$150,000 mainframe, less than half of a $25,000 minicomputer), a reporter could pore over digitized government records to tell complex narratives. As Jaspin noted, "Ten years ago, if you didn't have a mainframe computer, you were sunk." That had changed, and had thus changed journalism.[13] See Figure 5.1.

But part of the challenge of the new "computer-assisted reporting," that is, reporting done on and through PCs, was access to the databases and government records that made such reporting matter. Another challenge was whether or not reporters had access to even partially digitized records at their own publications, to aid with research. Data from *Editor & Publisher Yearbooks* and its *Market Guides* included that in 1990, on 105 of the largest-circulation U.S. dailies, with a median circulation of 193,445, and median staff of 193, about 70 had at least some kind of digital archive, with 64 percent giving reporters access to PCs for their day-to-day work. Some 73 papers, however, did not have a keyword-driven public-information-oriented database, and therefore lacked the ability to readily share resources, or allow outside researchers to easily collaborate.[14]

Proprietary database systems were increasingly available for newspapers starting in the mid- to late 1970s, and by the 1980s were within range of larger newspaper's technology budgets, but could still be expensive. A "full-text retrieval library system" by Atex, with a 410-megabyte hard drive and four dedicated VDTs, could cost about $200,000 to buy and install ($493,000 in 2018).[15] Databases and access to them remained big business through the 1990s. One expert believed that "on-line information services" could be worth up to $9.6 billion in 1992.[16] Accessing research databases was a truly expensive challenge through the 1970s and into the 1980s, but gradually became more affordable by the early 1990s. News organizations were not immune to these high barriers for entry, however. Access to data had once been so pricey, in fact, that reporters and editors had to have a good idea of where to look, and what to look at, beforehand, in order to avoid big charges.[17] A further challenge remained the ersatz and sometimes opaque way local and federal government offices tended to collect and store digital data. There were up to 125,000 computers dedicated to saving records, up from about 3,000 in 1966, when the Freedom of Information Act was first passed.[18]

Still, despite these obstacles, many observers felt that the barriers to entry would continue to lower, and editors at smaller newspapers, including Mary Ann Chick Whiteside at the *Flint Journal*, in Michigan, felt that "computers will be a routine tool used by all good journalists on daily stories as well as projects."[19] A small collection of textbooks, seminars and educators were helping to spread the necessary know-how to take advantage of reporting with PCs.[20]

A pioneering case in 1989 involved the use of government reports to cover the national scope of assault-weapon-related violence. Cox Newspapers correspondents James Stewart and Andrew Alexander negotiated access to crudely stored Bureau of Alcohol, Tobacco, and Firearms (ATF) records in Maryland. In exchange for the use of "trace forms," used to track the involvement of guns in crimes, Stewart and Alexander used software to privatize the records and thus adhere to federal privacy laws.

Some 42,758 trace forms, or about 800,000 separate data points, were entered via keyboard over a period from January 1988 to March 1989, using six rented IBM PCs, each with a 20-megabyte hard drive, and with help from six temporary workers.[21] These data were analyzed by a firm in Atlanta (which had an IBM mainframe). The resulting information was used for a series of stories in May 1989, later used by Congress members to support new gun laws. It was among the first computerized, non-governmental databases of gun violence.

As Jaspin, the expert in computer-assisted reporting, noted at the time, "We're at a funny juncture right now. While there is a lot that is computerized, not everything is computerized."[22]

Resistance and change in PC-powered newsrooms

In a recurring column by the president of the Center for Foreign Journalists and a retired editor of the *Boston Globe*, Thomas Winship complained about the impact of computerization on newsroom camaraderie. While he was self-confessed to be "computer illiterate," he conceded at the outset that "there is no turning back to the typewriter-hot type days. The electronic newsroom has wrought too many miracles in production, cost savings, speed and efficiency."

But that very efficiency (including the ability to write stories and send them from a home office) had a number of downsides, including allowing more journalists to work outside the newsroom. Peter Gammons, a baseball sports writer for *Sports Illustrated*, could work from home and did not have to go in to the newsroom.

"When the stars don't come to the office, it greatly diminishes the spirit, atmosphere and inspiration of the newsroom, especially for the young journalists who learn so much by schmoozing with those who have made it."[23]

Winship suggested that access to databases, archives and other resources should be limited for those who did not come in, and complained that "two-way electronic messaging puts a dent in group discussions and bull sessions in and out of the workplace."

Quoting Arthur Gelb, the then recently retired managing editor of the *New York Times*, who said that "reporters talk to computers rather than to each other," and how they had socialized more before, especially after work, Winship agreed, and said that "it is just too easy for an editor to message instructions to a reporter or photographer rather than to get up off his backside and walk across the room to discuss a story in a give-and-take" conversation.[24]

As Winship put it, "what an easy way out it is for reporters or editors to vent their feelings via message rather than have a face-to-face confrontation. Editors should tell their people to talk to each other, not only to their computer screen."

He added that with editing, working on a screen made it too easy to delete words permanently, or over-edit copy, versus editing with a paper and pencil. Winship *did* concede that Ellen Goodman, a syndicated columnist, might still have a point when she argued that "there is a lively computer culture out there . . . Messages are flying all over the lot."

She liked the quieter newsroom spaces of the early 1990s, which Winship decidedly did not, and he only half-seriously suggested that "some snappy human resources v.p. [vice president] . . . pipe over a newsroom p.a. [*sic*] system ink-scented tape beating out sounds of clattering typewriters, interspersed with shouts of, 'copy, copy' and 'boy, boy'."[25]

Writing a few years before, John W. Newton, a former newspaper staff member on the Peekskill, New York, *Evening Star* and the *New York Journal-American*, wrote about a similar phenomenon affecting more production-minded news workers. Thanks to desktop terminals, proofreaders' signs were becoming more and more unfamiliar, and "those who can read those symbols will be as scarce as handsewn buttonholes." He was worried that soon there would be "a generation of newspaper people . . . who'll never know how to indicate all caps, indents, transpositions, interlineations or other signs on copy."[26]

As editing became more screen-based, "There's a sadness there, the missing part, something more recent guys and dolls in the game will never experience."[27] Layout via software versus layout on analog devices just did not foster the same level of daily interactions, Newton said.

In his words, "The printer's old attitude of 'I'll give you a hand, partner,' when a lad, who didn't know quite where the hell box was, needed a little guidance around the composing room."

There was also an impact on reporter and editor engagement with mechanical-room staff, with no longer as much of a need for "the editorial people [to] knock a few back with the printers." Being able to save space on headlines, the spacing of the words on the page and even the overall aesthetic impact of text had meant that deadlines brought together editorial and production workers.

> Through it all editorial types have kept their cool and printers have turned to other chores for their living, with machines making corrections, changes and deletions without those proofs with those odd tracks scratches all over them in spidery lines. . . . But it was nice on a late day in winter to find a printer or two behind a distant Linotype enjoying some early holiday warmth with an editorial pal after the final deadline emergency had passed.

And with the passing of that needed interaction, something intangible had been lost, along with newspaper factory camaraderie, he said. "Those all-efficient men of lead and ink, many experts on the more abstract questions of English grammar, are no more. And Mr. Etaoin Shrdlu [a warning from the days of 'hot type'] is forever gone."[28]

Nostalgic reflections on previous generations of technology and work were of course nothing new in the trade press (going back at least to the last turn of the century and laments about the rise of the Linotype and the slow decline in the need for handset type and proofreaders). But there was definitely a notable shift observed by contemporaries on the transition to computerized techniques on all levels of production. It felt faster, more abrupt, and perhaps more complete.

Notes

1 Edward Miller, "Where Is Design Leading Us? It Can Help Bring Meaning to the Reader," *Quill*, Sept. 1992, 24–25.
2 Miller, "Where Is Design Leading Us?," 24–25.
3 Miller, "Where Is Design Leading Us?," 24–25.
4 This can be seen in the multiple editions of textbooks such as Tim Harrower's *The Newspaper Designer's Handbook*, first published by the Oregonian Publishing Company in 1989.
5 Peter Winter, "Digital Mania: Color Production Potential of the Personal Computer Is Explored," *Editor & Publisher*, Sept. 26, 1987, 6, 22.
6 Jim Rosenberg, "SII Ports Coyote to OS/2: Systems Vendor Rounds Out Standard-Platform Product Line with New Coyotes Going into Washington Post and Daily Oklahoman," *Editor & Publisher*, June 8, 1991, 14, 92.
7 For more on how corporate America's mindset impacted newsroom management practices, see Doug Underwood, *When MBAs Rule the Newsroom: How the Marketers and Managers Are Reshaping Today's Media* (New York: Columbia University Press, 1993).

8 Anonymous staff writer, "On the Supply Side . . ." *Editor & Publisher*, June 6, 1987, 86.

9 Neil H. Reisner, "Plugging into Cyberspace," *Columbia Journalism Review* (May/June 1992): 61–64; see also Katie Hafner, "The Epic Saga of the Well," *Wired*, May 1, 1997, www.wired.com/1997/05/ff-well/.

10 Will Mari, "(Electronic) Mailing the Editor: Early Use of Emails and Message Boards by Newspaper Readers in the 1980s and 1990s," paper presented at the Communication History division of the International Communication Association in Prague, Czech Republic, May 2018.

11 George Landau, "Quantum Leaps: Computer Journalism Takes Off," *Columbia Journalism Review* (May/June 1992): 61–64.

12 Landau, "Quantum Leaps: Computer Takes Off," 61.

13 Tess Chichioco, "Sophisticated PCs Aid in Gathering Information," *Editor & Publisher*, Sept. 2, 1989, 21. Chichioco notes that PCs themselves had come a long way since the early 1980s; for between $1,000 and $3,000, a reporter could have access to a PC with up to about 300 megabytes of memory, crucial for analyzing thousands of pages of documents stored digitally. Jaspin noted, too, that an early use of computers for reporting was in 1967, when the *Detroit Free Press* used a mainframe to "tabulate information from a huge public-opinion poll following the riots," and then another was when the *Philadelphia Inquirer* used a mainframe to search data from public records about racial bias in the justice system, in about 1972; more on these examples in chapter 2. See also "Kansas City Star Begins In-Depth Test of PCs," *Editor & Publisher*, June 21, 1986, 46. The *Boston Globe* was using "computer access to IRS files to produce investigative news reporters" in the mid-1980s.

14 Jean Ward and Kathleen A. Hansen, "Newspapers and Electronic Technologies: Study Covers Commercial Databases, Electronic Libraries, PCs and Portable Computers, and Fax Machines at 105 Newspapers," *Editor & Publisher*, Nov. 3, 1990, 34–36. Ward and Hansen supplemented their trade-press data with a 92-item questionnaire, along with interviews, to get a sense of computer use in U.S. newsrooms.

15 Anonymous staff writer, "Basis Library System Offered by Atex," *Editor & Publisher*, Feb. 4, 1984, 4. Some newspapers developed their own, in-house systems, and either scanned material via OCR and stored the images, or cataloged files in a keyword, or index-based, database, that allowed for faster searching of hard-copy material. Some of these early systems were reviewed by Anthony Smith in his *Goodbye Gutenberg*, covered in the second chapter of this study.

16 Donna Demac, "Database Dollars: Whose Are They?," *Columbia Journalism Review* (Sept./Dec. 1992): 21. Demac, the director of the Program on Copyright & the New Technologies at New York University's Interactive Telecommunications Program, pointed out that the issues of rights management, especially in regards to freelancers and contributors to such services, could be a further sticking point.

17 L.M. Boyd, "A Small Syndicate Goes Electronic," *Editor & Publisher*, Mar. 3, 1979, 28; the AP's DataFeature service, at $4 per week per feature per paper, with the UPI also charging a "use of computer" charge of $100 a week, along with $2,200 for a "black box" to connect to a Ascii-software-running terminal, with $1 per week per take (about 1,000 words, according to Boyd) per paper, for its rival service. See also Andrew Radolf, "News Research Service Opens Computer Center," *Editor & Publisher*, Oct. 4, 1980, 18; Lexis-Nexis (the former for legal data, the latter for news), charged $50 a month plus fees

from $1 to $1.50 per minute in 1980; terminals would cost $20 a month for a small desk model or $150 for a more advanced terminal. See also "NEXIS," *Columbia Journalism Review* (May/June 1984): 28; an ad for NEXIS, "the world's largest electronic library of news and business information" listed a rate of $20 an hour (down from $90); you could also search individual files for $9 per file access could be obtained by using an IBM PC, an IBM Displaywriter, IBM 3101 terminal or TeleVideo 950 terminal.

18 Anonymous staff writer, "Bury It in the Computer," *Editor & Publisher*, July 15, 1989, 4.

19 Mary Ann Chick Whiteside, "Computers – Not Just Another Reporting Tool," *Editor & Publisher*, Nov. 2, 1991, 1, 20.

20 Mary Ann Chick Whiteside, "Resources for Computer-Assisted Journalism," *Editor & Publisher*, Nov. 2, 1991, 2, 4. Some of the textbooks include *The Reporter's Handbook: An Investigator's Guide to Documents and Techniques*, published by Investigative Reporters & Editors (IRE) in 1991, and costing $19, along with Philip Meyer's already then-classic, *Precision Journalism: A Reporter's Guide*, first published in 1973, but updated in 1978 and then in 1991, and costing $12.95 for the paperback version, published by Indiana. See also Mary Ann Chick Whiteside, "Getting Started in Computer-Assisted Journalism," *Editor & Publisher*, Nov. 2, 1991, 5, 6. The changing definitions and uses of technology, along with the rhetoric used to frame and conceptualize such technology tools, would be worthy of their own study.

21 Tess Chichioco, "Computer-Assisted Reporting: Newspapers Are Beginning to Use It to Their Advantage," *Editor & Publisher*, Sept. 2, 1989, 20–21.

22 Chichioco, "Computer-Assisted Reporting," 20–21. The total cost to rent the computers and pay the workers reached about $10,000.

23 Thomas Winship, "The New Curmudgeon," *Editor & Publisher*, Aug. 3, 1991, 3. Complaining about the absence (or presence) of newsroom "stars," including columnists, was an old refrain, incidentally, dating back to the earlier part of the century, with telephone technology contributing to the "untethering" (and sometimes also the opposite) of reporters and some editors from having to stay in the same building to do their work.

24 Winship, "The New Curmudgeon," 3. Gelb was specifically referring to the ways that different tribal groups (copy editors, reporters, etc.) in the newsroom would meet after work in bars and restaurants.

25 Winship, "The New Curmudgeon," 3. Otherwise newsrooms were beginning to feel, at least to critics like Winship, more like insurance offices; prior to typewriters, while newsrooms were noisy, they were also less loud than they had been from the 1880s through the 1970s.

26 John W. Newton, "Shop Talk at Thirty: The All-Efficient Desktop Terminal Has Eliminated Camaraderie with the Backshop," *Editor & Publisher*, June 10, 1989, 56, 146.

27 Even the way he frames the process is interesting, in how writing on a screen, even a decade or so into more commonly accessible word processors, was a fairly alien experience:

> Today an editor calls up the story in question, pushes little keys, makes a cursor obediently follow his command, then interpolates, deletes, transposes, writes heads optically enlarged to fit the space planned for that yarn, and it's off to the races.
>
> That, rather than using a caret to indicate a letter or word insertion; triple underline for caps; circling for the spelling of an abbreviation or circling a

full word to indicate its shortening; the oddly curlicued or boxlike transpose flourish that depended upon user mood for its final form; the three-em dash some editors called "jim" dashes; and the breaking up of endless paragraphs crafted by verbose writers into terse, always compelling paragraphs by a journeyman rewrite man or reporter.

28 Newton, "Shop Talk at Five Thirty," *Editor & Publisher*, 56, 146. Also see David W. Dunlap, "1978: 'Farewell, Etaoin Shrdlu'," *New York Times*, Nov. 13, 2014, www.nytimes.com/times-insider/2014/11/13/1978-farewell-etaoin-shrdlu/. "Often, when Linotype operators made a mistake, they would run a finger down the first two rows to produce the words 'etaoin shrdlu' in the line of type; a clear warning to printers that it should be discarded."

6   Conclusion
The mid-1990s and what came after

Beginning in the mid-1990s, the civilian internet would gradually usher in more and deeper disruptions for the newspaper industry than computerization ever really did. Some of these would not be felt for years, as with the decline in classified ads and the challenge of making money from their on-line counterparts, but some would be felt faster, as with increased and immediate reader interactions, and reporters and editors who could write faster, more thoroughly and more cheaply and in real time in ways that allowed them to compete with their traditional rivals in TV and radio.

Some of these news workers would go to help launch, in time, their own fully on-line ventures, such as the early internet-based magazines *Slate* and *Salon*, or hybrid on-line ventures, including the web sites for newspapers like the *San Jose Mercury News*, *Newsday*, the *Detroit Free Press*, the *Kansas City Star*, the *Spokesman-Review*, the *Fort Worth Star-Telegram* and others. As early as late 1993 and early 1994, nearly 20 major metropolitan newspapers had some kind of Web-enabled access.[1] PC-based reporting was increasingly common, and access to the internet and email was considered increasingly normal, if still fairly novel for day-to-day reporting.[2]

The tendency to give away stories sans paywalls or other subscription-based services would inculcate an entire generation against paying for curated, researched journalism, and is only now changing for the better as multiple revenue streams start to stabilize parts of the industry. Perhaps the percentage of readers who really read the news on the internet was so not-impactful on traditional ad revenues for so long (right through the mid-2000s) that the temptation to merely supplement the print product for free was just too great. Much more on the gradual and sometimes economically painful transition to the Web can and should be written.

And yet working with computers with layout, editing and reporting was the norm, even if the business of journalism was in for an intense series of separate economic disruptions starting in the late 1990s, including the impact of Craigslist.

"Any journalist who has been retired for ten years or even less would hardly recognize the newsroom now," wrote Paul Williams, a British journalist who had helped the *Daily Telegraph*'s newsroom computerization process, in 1990. Working with smart terminals was simply part of the day's routine. "No more the clatter of ancient typewriters . . . perhaps just a couple remain, left behind to type out envelopes or expense forms. Instead there is a forest of video screens and the gentle clacking of keyboards . . . altogether it is a quieter place."[3]

Only about 12 years before, OCR technology and VDTs had lived side by side, and while the latter were "more readily and graciously received in the newsroom" due to their more intuitive interface, many reporters and editors still relied on hard copies of their material.[4] The more interesting question for at least some researchers, even in the midst of the changes of the 1960s, 1970s and later the 1980s and early 1990s, was what would happen to the work routines of news workers, and to the field itself, as timescales shrank, more and more detailed contextualizing information became available and the use of computers was routinized in many – though not all – newsrooms by fits and starts.[5]

Despite the general, if not necessarily fated, move to a computerized newsroom right up to the beginning of the commercial internet, the media historian cannot work also as a prophet, comfortably, when it comes to predicting what will happen with the continued disruptions of technology on journalism as a field. That caution being noted, however, if history remains a rough guide, it takes something like 30 years to get a handle on what, exactly, a new means of news delivery means for paying the bills. Newsroom computerization is no exception, and was a long and messy process.

After all, it took at least a solid two decades for even the savviest, most generous and forward-thinking publishers, and arguably large organizations such as the ANPA, to figure out what, exactly, newsroom computerization was good for, along with the utility of related technologies such as digital photography, mobile reporting and databases and networks.[6] Working with the brightest minds of the day at MIT, the ANPA still had been forced to make a number of bets on technologies, some of which either were dead ends or just did not last very long, instead becoming transitory tools at best (including OCR).

A reporter, possibly turned editor, whose career spanned the time period covered by this study witnessed seismically disruptive changes, losing some control over aspects of his or her work (having to write more every day) but also gaining a great deal of additional autonomy and ability (not having to schlep oneself to the newspaper's paper archive, or rely as much on conjecture). This latter function of newsroom computerization did mean, as media-tech prognosticators like Bagdikian and Smith believed, that newspapers could move beyond their industrial capacities and become more truly pathfinders of the burgeoning information economy. Before Google and Amazon (though not quite before Apple and Microsoft), journalism pushed the boundaries of what was possible with information technology.

Lost, perhaps, in narratives about the rise of the internet in the 1990s, then, is this backstory, the immediately pre-internet interregnum. From analog-digital to more truly digital, from newsroom mainframes, then mini-computers and then microprocessors, technology changed what news workers could do, how fast they could do it and where they could do it from.

If one were to sketch the rise of computer technology in journalism from a tech-deterministic perspective, the impact of machines on speed, accuracy and access to data was perhaps seemingly inevitable. Especially in the early information economy pioneered by news, mainframes, minicomputers and then microprocessors disrupted routines and built new ones, yes, but they also built on older concepts such as timeliness, in vogue since the telegraph and the typewriter in the 1880s.[7]

From a social-shaping or social constructionist point of view, news workers' values such as timeliness actually drove the adoption of computer tools in equally powerful ways, even with fairly esoteric (for the time, at least) devices such as digital cameras, databases and portable (later mobile) computers in the form of laptops and, later, cell- and smartphones. In this narrative, news workers, far from being the victims of computer technologies, were active agents in their own fate, choosing some machines over others, sometimes due to a lack of audience interest (i.e., with Videotex and Teletext services) or familiarity (some reporters preferred the sound and even feel of computer keyboards over some kinds of electronic typewriters, became the former reminded them of well-oiled mechanical typewriters).[8]

Of course, news workers could feel, at least, that they were at the mercy of new tech tools, especially some of the production workers whose devices were digitized. Their experiences should not be dismissed, and they are relevant today when contemplating what software tools are already doing to some forms of routinized news, such as sports and business stories. As artificial intelligence enters an already turbulent journalism industry, much more disruption is likely in store.

But the ability to reskill or multiskill, or pursue previously unknown jobs (such as that of the layout editor, beginning in the 1980s and early 1990s with new software tools), should also not be dismissed.[9] And if media history, in particular, is any guide to understanding current disruptions, it does show that reporters and editors are resilient and creative, even if business models and tech tools continue to change their occupation and even if their newsrooms transform into even more disbursed, nimble organizations out of necessity.

Any history of disruptive technology tools should consider the agency and voice of the people experiencing them. With that admonition in mind, I hope I have done the same for the era from about the 1950s through the early 1990s. What came next with newsroom computerization, namely, the rise of the internet, deserves its own story.

Notes

1 Jack D. Lail, "Newspapers Online: Electronic Delivery Is Hot . . . Again," *Quill*, Jan./Feb. 1994, 39–44.

2 See, for example, John S. Makulowich, "Internet: Explore the Network of Networks," *Quill*, Sept. 1993, 28; John S. Makulowich, "Email: Make Contact Without Playing Phone Tag," *Quill*, Sept. 1993, 29; Jack Lail, "Computer Journalism: It's Where There Is the Largest Gap Between What People Know and What They Need to Know," *Quill*, Sept. 1993, 22; but also, David Noack, "Letters to the Editor Via Email: Some Papers Let Readers Use a High-Tech Method of Corresponding," *Editor & Publisher*, June 25, 1994, 40; Bob Andelman, "An Advance Look at Tampa Bay Online: With the Tampa Tribune's New On-Line Service Set to Debut in August on Prodigy, the Newpaper's Deputy Managing Editor for Electronic Publishing Provides Some Insight on How It Will Work," *Editor & Publisher*, June 25, 1994. It is fascinating to see how perception of the internet's potential, and the ability to interact with users via the web, was so positive in the early to mid-1990s. It would take a decade for a complex, and turbulent, narrative to emerge with the demise of classified ads and the rise of on-line hate speech. Still, for most of the 1990s, the internet as a set of technologies represented hope, and not anxiety, for news workers. That only may now, gradually, be changing again.

3 Paul Williams, *The Computerized Newspaper: A Practical Guide for Systems Users* (Oxford: Heinemann Professional Publishing Ltd., 1990), 5.

4 Dineh Moghdam, *Computers in Newspaper Publishing: User-Oriented Systems* (New York: Marcel Dekker, Inc., 1978), 85–86.

5 Nancy Carter and John Cullen, *Computerization of Newspaper Organizations: The Impact of Technology on Organizational Structuring* (Lanham, MD: University Press of America, 1983), 5.

6 As reviewed in the first couple of chapters of this study, the partnership with MIT, while on the surface fairly improbable, makes sense if one remembers the 20 percent or higher profit margins enjoyed by metropolitan-newspaper owners, regardless of whether or not they were families, like the Ochs Sulzbergers of the *New York Times*, the Chandlers of the *Los Angeles Times*, or the Grahams of the *Washington Post* (now inherited by the Bezos family?), or chains such as Scripps-Howard, Knight-Ridder or Hearst.

7 Richard Kielbowicz, "Regulating Timeliness: Technologies, Laws, and the News, 1840–1970," *Journalism and Communication Monographs* 17 (Spring 2015): 5–83. See also Mike Ananny, "Networked News Time: How Slow – or Fast – Do Publics Need News to Be?" *Digital Journalism*, published online Feb. 2016. 1–18; Ford Risley, "Newspapers and Timeliness," *American Journalism* 17, no. 4 (2000): 97–103.

8 Marty Sutphin, "Plug in to a Terminal: Faster, Neater and More Error-Free," *Quill*, Nov. 1973, 25–26. "It has more the feel of a manual typewriter. Most newsmen, accosted to pounding a battered but comfortable manual typewriter, have an intense distaste for electric typewriters. One of the pleasant surprises for them is that the electronic CRT keyboard does not feel like an electric," 26.

9 And again, as Örnebring has argued, is not a simple narrative of decline and fall, nor one of unfettered triumph, but some messy middle in between; see his "Technology and Journalism-as-Labor: Historical Perspectives," *Journalism* 11, no. 57 (2010): 57–74.

Bibliography and notes on sources

Trade publications and other primary-source journals[1]

American Newspaper Publishers Association (ANPA) *News Research Bulletin*
Columbia Journalism Review
Editor & Publisher
Editor & Publisher International Yearbook
Newspaper Research Journal (Newspaper Division of the Association for Education in Journalism and Mass Communication)
Nieman Reports (Nieman Foundation for Journalism at Harvard University)
The Quill (Sigma Delta Chi [SDC], i.e., the Society of Professional Journalists [SPJ])
Washington Journalism Review (later the *American Journalism Review*)

Archives and primary sources consulted[2]

Bagdikian, Ben H. *The Information Machines: Their Impact on Men and the Media.* New York: Harper & Row, 1971.

Carter, Nancy M., and John Cullen. *Computerization of Newspaper Organizations: The Impact of Technology on Organizational Structuring.* Lanham, MD: University Press of America, 1983.

Compaine, Benjamin M. *The Newspaper Industry in the 1980s: An Assessment of Economics and Technology.* White Plains, NY: Knowledge Industry Publications, Inc., 1980.

Hynds, Ernest. *American Newspapers in the 1980s.* New York: Hastings House Publishers, 1980.

Living Computer Museum Collection, Seattle, Washington.

Moghdam, Dineh. *Computers in Newspaper Publishing: User-Oriented Systems.* New York: Marcel Dekker, Inc., 1978.

"The Need for a Competitive and Diverse Electronic Publishing Market," testimony given before the U.S. Senate Sub-committee on Communication, Dec. 11, 1987, Washington, D.C.

Overhage, Carl F. J., and R. Joyce Harman, eds. *INTREX: Report of a Planning Conference on Information Transfer Experiments.* Cambridge, MA: MIT Press, 1965.

Smith, Anthony. *Goodbye Gutenberg: The Newspaper Revolution of the 1980s*. New York: Oxford University Press, 1980.

Williams, Paul. *The Computerized Newspaper: A Practical Guide for Systems Users*. Oxford: Heinemann Professional Publishing Ltd., 1990.

Secondary sources[3]

Abbott, Andrew. *The System of Professions: An Essay on the Division of Expert Labor*. Chicago: University of Chicago Press, 1988.

Ananny, Mike. "Networked News Time: How Slow – or Fast – Do Publics Need News to Be?" *Digital Journalism*. Published online Feb. 2016: 1–18.

Anderson, C. W., and Juliette De Maeyer. "Objects of Journalism and the News." *Journalism* 16, no. 1 (2014): 3–9.

Barnhurst, Kevin G., and John C. Nerone. *The Form of News: A History*. New York: Guilford Press, 2001.

Bijker, Wiebe E., Thomas Parke Hughes and Trevor Pinch. *The Social Construction of Technological Systems, Anniversary Edition: New Directions in the Sociology and History of Technology*. Cambridge, MA: MIT Press, 2012.

Boczkowski, Pablo J. *News at Work: Imitation in an Age of Information Abundance*. Chicago: University of Chicago Press, 2010.

Boczkowski, Pablo J. "The Material Turn in the Study of Journalism: Some Hopeful and Cautionary Remarks from an Early Explorer." *Journalism* 16, no. 1 (2015): 65–68.

Braverman, Harry. *Labor and Monopoly Capital: The Degradation of Work in the Twentieth Century*. New York: Monthly Review Press, 1974.

Breed, Warren. "Social Control in the Newsroom: A Functional Analysis." *Social Forces* 33, no. 4 (1955): 326–335.

Bureau of Labor Statistics, U.S. Dept. of Labor. "CPI Inflation Calculator." Accessed Oct. 22, 2018. www.bls.gov/data/inflation_calculator.htm.

Campbell-Kelly, Martin. *From Airline Reservations to Sonic the Hedgehog: A History of the Software Industry*. Cambridge, MA: MIT Press, 2003.

Carlson, Matt. *Journalistic Authority: Legitimizing News in the Digital Era*. New York: Columbia University Press, 2017.

Ceruzzi, Paul E. *A History of Modern Computing*. Cambridge, MA: MIT Press, 2003.

Chandler, Alfred D., Jr. *The Visible Hand: The Managerial Revolution in American Business*. Cambridge, MA: The Belknap Press, 1977.

Coopersmith, Jonathan. *Faxed: The Rise and Fall of the Fax Machine*. Baltimore, MD: Johns Hopkins University Press, 2016.

Cortada, James W. *A Bibliographic Guide to the History of Computing, Computers, and the Information Processing Industry*. New York: Greenwood Press, 1990.

Cortada, James W. *A Bibliographic Guide to the History of Computer Applications, 1950–1990*. Westport, CT: Greenwood Press, 1996.

Cortada, James W., ed. *Rise of the Knowledge Worker. Resources for the Knowledge-Based Economy*. Boston: Butterworth-Heinemann, 1998.

Cortada, James W. *Before the Computer: IBM, NCR, Burroughs, and Remington Rand and the Industry They Created, 1865–1956*. Princeton, NJ: Princeton University Press, 2000.

Cortada, James W. *The Digital Hand: Volume II, How Computers Changed the Work of American Financial, Telecommunications, Media, and Entertainment Industries*. New York: Oxford University Press, 2006.

Creech, Brian. "A Newsmaker's Tool: The 35mm Camera and Journalism's Material Epistemology." *Journalism* 18, no. 9 (2017): 1125–1141.

Deuze, Mark. "What Is Journalism? Professional Identity and Ideology of Journalists Reconsidered." *Journalism* 6, no. 4 (2005): 442–464.

Dooley, Patricia L. *Taking Their Political Place: Journalists and the Making of an Occupation*. Westport, CT: Greenwood Press, 1997.

Dunlap, David W. "Looking Back: 'Farewell, Etaoin Shrdlu'." *New York Times*, Nov. 13, 2014. Accessed Oct. 25, 2018. www.nytimes.com/times-insider/2014/11/13/1978-farewell-etaoin-shrdlu/.

Earl, Jennifer, and Katrina Kimport. *Digitally Enabled Social Change: Activism in the Internet Age*. Cambridge, MA: MIT Press, 2011.

Edwards, Richard. *Contested Terrain: The Transformation of the Workplace in the Twentieth Century*. New York: Basic Books, 1979.

Eisenstein, Elizabeth. *The Printing Revolution in Early Modern Europe*. Cambridge: University of Cambridge Press, 2005.

Ekbia, Hamid R., and Bonnie A. Nardi. *Heteromation: And Other Stories of Computing and Capitalism*. Cambridge, MA: MIT Press, 2017.

Evans, Claire L. *Broad Band: The Untold Story of the Women Who Made the Internet*. New York: Penguin Random House, 2018.

Friedman, Barbara. "Editor's Note: Is That a Thing? The Twitching Document and the Talking Object." *American Journalism* 31, no. 3 (2014): 307–311.

Gitelman, Lisa, and Geoffrey B. Pingree, eds. *New Media, 1740–1915. Media in Transition*. Cambridge, MA: MIT Press, 2003.

Goddard, Michael. "Opening Up the Black Boxes: Media Archeology, Anarchaeology and Media Materiality." *New Media & Society* 17, no. 11 (2015): 1761–1776.

Hafner, Katie. "The Epic Saga of the Well." *Wired*, May 1, 1997. Accessed Oct. 27, 2018. www.wired.com/1997/05/ff-well/.

Hafner, Katie, and Matthew Lyon. *Where Wizards Stay Up Late: The Origins of the Internet*. New York: Simon and Schuster, 2006.

Hallin, Daniel C. "Commercialism and Professionalism in the American News Media." In *Mass Media and Society*, edited by James Curran and Michael Gurevitch, 242–260. London: Arnold, 2000.

Hardt, Hanno, and Bonnie Brennen, eds. *Newsworkers: Toward a History of the Rank and File*. Minneapolis: University of Minnesota Press, 1995.

John, Richard R. and Jonathan Silberstein-Loeb, eds. *Making News: The Political Economy of Journalism in Britain and America from the Glorious Revolution to the Internet*. New York: Oxford University Press, 2015.

Jones, Charles R. *Facsimile*. New York: Rinehart Books, Inc., 1949.

Keith, Susan. "Horseshoes, Stylebooks, Wheels, Poles, and Dummies: Objects of Editing Power in 20th-Century Newsrooms." *Journalism* 16, no. 1 (2015): 44–60.

Kielbowicz, Richard B. "Regulating Timeliness: Technologies, Laws, and the News, 1840–1970." *Journalism & Communication Monographs* 17, no. 1 (2015): 5–83.

Kirschenbaum, Matthew. *Track Changes: A Literary History of Word Processing.* Cambridge, MA: Harvard University Press, 2016.

Kline, Ronald, and Trevor Pinch. "Users as Agents of Technological Change: The Social Construction of the Automobile in the Rural United States." *Technology and Culture* 37, no. 4 (1996): 763–795.

MacDougall, Robert. *The People's Network: The Political Economy of the Telephone in the Gilded Age.* Philadelphia: University of Pennsylvania Press, 2014.

Mailland, Julien, and Kevin Mailland. *Minitel: Welcome to the Internet.* Cambridge, MA: MIT Press, 2017.

Mari, Will. "The American Newsroom: A Social History, 1920 to 1960." Ph.D. dissertation, University of Washington, 2016.

Mari, Will. "Technology in the Newsroom: Adoption of the Telephone and the Radio Car from *c.* 1920 to 1960." *Journalism Studies* 19, no. 9 (2018): 1366–1389.

Meyer, Philip. *Precision Journalism: A Reporter's Introduction to Social Science Methods.* Bloomington: Indiana University Press, 1973.

Meyer, Philip. *The New Precision Journalism.* Bloomington: Indiana University Press, 1991.

Nerone, John, and Kevin G. Barnhurst. "U.S. Newspaper Types, the Newsroom, and the Division of Labor, 1750–2000." *Journalism Studies* 4, no. 4 (2003): 435–449.

Örnebring, Henrik. "Technology and Journalism-as-Labor: Historical Perspectives." *Journalism* 11, no. 57 (2010): 57–74.

Peters, Benjamin. "And Lead Us Not into Thinking the New Is New: A Bibliographic Case for New." *New Media and Society* 11, no. 13 (2009): 13–30.

Peters, Benjamin. *How Not to Network a Nation: The Uneasy History of the Soviet Internet.* Cambridge, MA: MIT Press, 2017.

Pool, Ithiel De Sola. *Technologies of Freedom: On Free Speech in an Electronic Age.* Cambridge, MA: The Belknap Press, 1983.

Rid, Thomas. *Rise of the Machines: The Lost History of Cybernetics.* London: Scribe Publications, 2016.

Risley, Ford. "Newspapers and Timeliness." *American Journalism* 17, no. 4 (2000): 97–103.

Roessner, Amber, Rick Popp, Brian Creech and Fred Blevens. " 'A Measure of Theory?' Considering the Role of Theory in Media History." *American Journalism* 30, no. 2 (2013): 260–278.

Schudson, Michael. *Discovering the News: A Social History of American Newspapers.* New York: Basic Books, 1978.

Schudson, Michael. "What Sorts of Things Are Thingy? And What Sorts of Thinginess Are There? Notes on Stuff and Social Construction." *Journalism* 16, no. 1 (2015): 61–64.

Shoemaker, Pamela J., and Stephen D. Reese. *Mediating the Message in the 21st Century: A Media Sociology Perspective.* 3rd ed. New York: Routledge, Taylor & Francis Group, 2014.

Starr, Paul. "Reading: Old and New." *Daedalus* 112, no. 1 (1983): 143–156.

Streeter, Thomas. *The Net Effect: Romance, Capitalism, and the Internet.* New York: New York University Press, 2011.

Underwood, Doug. *When MBAs Rule the Newsroom: How the Marketers and Managers Are Reshaping Today's Media*. New York: Columbia University Press, 1993.

Usher, Nikki. *Making News at the New York Times*. Ann Arbor, MI: University of Michigan Press, 2014.

Weaver, David H. *Videotex Journalism: Teletext, Viewdata, and the News*. Hillsdale, NJ: Lawrence Erlbaum Associates, Inc., 1983.

Wolton, Dominique. *L'information Demain de la Presse Écrite aux Nouveaux Médias*. Avec J-L. Lepigeon. Paris, France: La Documentation Française, 1979.

Notes

1 As also noted in the introduction, nearly every available issue of *Quill* and *Columbia Journalism Review* was examined from *c.* 1960 to 1992 and *c.* 1961 to 1992, respectively. Every issue of *Editor & Publisher* from 1958 to 1960 was read to establish a baseline, and then a representative sample of a progressive issue (first, second, third, fourth, etc. per month, or one issue per month) was read from *c.* 1970 to 1977, then 1984–1992, with a few issues consulted in 1993–1994, to bound the study; selected issues were also consulted from 1993 to 1994 for *Quill* to confirm that that year was a turning point for early internet adoption by newspapers. Note that approximately every other issue of *Editor & Publisher* was read from *c.* 1977 through 1983, as that was an especially crucial juncture in newsroom computerization. The yearbooks for 1975, 1980 and 1990 were consulted for *Editor & Publisher International Yearbook*. With the *Newspaper Research Journal*, founded in 1979, the years from *c.* 1984 to 1992 were examined more closely. The latter's being indexed assisted with this more scholarly source. ANPA's *News Research Bulletin*, affiliated loosely with the ANPA *Research Bulletin* (summaries of which also often appeared in *Editor & Publisher*), was consulted for the years from *c.* 1973 to 1977. Future research projects will look more directly at the *Bulletin*, as it is a rich source for information on the Research Institute's industry-academic collaboration, particularly with MIT. Scattered issues of the *Washington Journalism Review* (later the *American Journalism Review*) served as a secondary check on *Quill* and *Columbia Journalism Review*. Along with *Newspaper Research Journal*, selected issues of *Nieman Reports* from *c.* 1978 to 1992 were consulted, and provided a helpful academic perspective on computerization. Finally, Stephen Waters's 1977 report on *Newsroom Computerization*, published by the ANPA, is also worth consulting, for researchers interested in the long computing interregnum of the latter Cold War.

2 "Primary" sources, versus more secondary sources, were consulted in their role (beyond the museum archives) here in their capacity as contemporary accounts on newsroom computerization.

3 While not all of these are cited in the manuscript, these authors contributed to the context and thinking required for its conceptualization, particularly for the era in question.

Index

Note: Page numbers in *italics* indicate a figure.

Printed in the United States
by Baker & Taylor Publisher Services